D0765308

JFK, WORLD WAR II, AND THE HEROIC RESCUE OF PT 109

IN HARM'S WAY

IAIN MARTIN

Scholastic Press / New York

★ ★ ★

Library of Congress Cataloging-in-Publication Data available

ISBN 978-1-338-18567-6

10 9 8 7 6 5 4 3 2 1   18 19 20 21 22

Printed in the U.S.A.   23
First edition, August 2018

Cover design by Christopher Stengel
Interior design by Kay Petronio

This book is dedicated to my father, Blair Robertson Martin, for teaching me a love of history

Eternal Father, strong to save,
Whose arm hath bound the restless wave,
Who bidd'st the mighty ocean deep,
Its own appointed limits keep;
Oh, hear us when we cry to Thee,
For those in peril on the sea!

—Navy Hymn

C·O·N·T·E·N·T·S

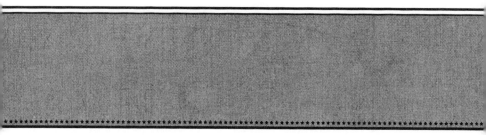

★ NAVAL RANKS IN WORLD WAR II ★

ENLISTED RANKS	★★★	OFFICER RANKS
Apprentice Seaman		Ensign
Seaman Second Class		Lieutenant Junior Grade (jg)
Seaman First Class		Lieutenant
Petty Officer Third Class		Lieutenant Commander
Petty Officer Second Class		Commander
Petty Officer First Class		Captain
Chief Petty Officer		Rear Admiral
		Vice Admiral
		Admiral
		Fleet Admiral

★ GLOSSARY OF NAVAL TERMS ★

aft—toward the stern (rear) of a boat or a ship

bow—the cutting edge of the hull at the front of a boat or a ship

destroyer—a fast, maneuverable warship designed to escort other ships

enlisted men—sailors or soldiers who are not officers

fore—the front section of a boat or a ship

knots—a measure of speed on water; 1 nautical knot equals 1.15 miles per hour

MTB Squadron—a group of up to twelve motor torpedo boats

PBY—an American Navy twin engine flying boat

port—to the left of a boat or a ship facing the bow

PT boat—patrol torpedo boat

skipper—the commander of a boat or a ship

starboard—to the right of a boat or a ship facing the bow

stern—the very end (rear) of a boat or a ship

PROLOGUE

O God, thy sea is so great
and my boat is so small.

—Breton fishermen's prayer

NANTUCKET SOUND, LATE AUGUST, 1930

John Fitzgerald Kennedy (Jack to his friends) knew they were in trouble when the waves started to crash over the bow of their tiny sailboat, drenching him and Kathleen, his younger sister. She was huddled up in her jacket, looking out for the next wave that might swamp them. Jack leaned into the tiller and kept his sails full of wind as they made their way toward home. He was just thirteen years old.

It had been a perfect late summer day when they left Hyannis Port bound for Osterville six miles away. On their way back, the weather had suddenly turned into a storm with darkening skies and growing seas. Yet the real danger

came from the fog—a dense "dungeon fog," as the local fishermen would call it. The fog crept in from the sea and blocked all sight of land from view.

If Jack made a mistake, if he wandered off course, if he failed to sight land, they could be blown out to sea. With no radio, no flare gun, no life vests, and only light jackets to ward off the cold, they wouldn't last long. Yet Jack was an expert sailor, and he knew these waters and the Cape Cod shoreline like the back of his hand.

Soon, out of the mist, Jack could see land: a beach, houses along the shore, and in the distance a pier, beyond which lay their family's summer home. Waiting for the children on the pier stood two figures in the mist, peering out to sea, looking for their sailboat. Jack and Kathleen knew who they were—their father and Joe Jr., their big brother. Jack had come through the squall, but it would not be the last time he faced danger at sea and saved those close to him.

Lieutenant John F. Kennedy in 1942, before he shipped out to the Pacific.

I Want YOU! for the U.S. Navy

I can imagine no more rewarding a career. And any man who may be asked in this century what he did to make his life worthwhile, I think I can respond with a good deal of pride and satisfaction: "I served in the United States Navy."

—President John F. Kennedy

UNITED STATES NAVY
Identification Card

KENNEDY, John F.
Name

John Kennedy
Signature

Color Hair Brown Eyes Green
Weight 150 Birth 5-29-1

Void after D.O.W.

LIEUT. USNR

N. Nav. 546 Vandgrift

John F. Kennedy (right) with his father, Joseph Kennedy Sr., and his older brother, Joseph Kennedy Jr., in Palm Beach, Florida, 1931.

CHAPTER 1

A FAST SHIP

*I wish to have no connection with
any ship that does not sail fast; for
I intend to go in harm's way.*

—Captain John Paul Jones, 1778

NANTUCKET SOUND, JULY 29, 1941

Eleven years later, Jack once again sailed on the Nantucket Sound, this time in his beloved twenty-five-foot sailboat *Victura*. Jack had chosen the name, a Latin word meaning "about to conquer." The boat had been a gift from his father to him and his brother Joe Jr. Together they had raced it many times and won several championships. Today, however, Jack was heading for the sailboat race at Edgartown, on Martha's Vineyard, with his lifelong friend Torbert Hart Macdonald.

Jack was now twenty-four years old. Both he and Joe Jr. were Harvard graduates, both outstanding young men at the start of promising adulthoods. Yet the brothers had put aside law school to volunteer for the navy. Joe was learning to fly bombers, and Jack had been assigned to Naval Intelligence in Washington, DC. War was coming. Everyone knew it was just a matter of time before the United States was drawn into the fight with Germany, Italy, and Japan. When the time came, the brothers wanted to serve.

As he sailed into the harbor, Jack noticed a type of boat he had never seen before at the pier. It was a navy patrol vessel. PT boats, as they were called, were elegant craft made from wood; this particular type was seventy-seven feet long and powered by three enormous Packard engines, each capable of 1,350 horsepower. At full throttle, they could reach speeds above forty knots (forty nautical knots equals forty-six miles per hour). Built for war, they were armed to the teeth with two twin .50-caliber heavy machine gun turrets and four torpedo tubes that held Mark VIII 21-inch torpedoes. They were the fastest and, for their size, the most heavily armed craft in the navy.

It wasn't just a PT boat's speed that impressed Jack. The boat was commanded by a junior officer, a lieutenant, which was only two ranks above Jack's rank of ensign. Unlike a larger warship where he would just be one of many junior

Who Was John F. Kennedy?

Jack arrived into the world on May 29, 1917, in his father's house at 83 Beals Street in Brookline, Massachusetts. Christened John Fitzgerald Kennedy after his grandfather, he was the second son of Joseph and Rose Kennedy. In addition to his older brother, Joseph Jr., there would be seven more siblings: Rosemary, Kathleen, Eunice, Patricia, Robert, Jean, and Edward. The Kennedys were Irish Catholics— loyal Americans, but often looked down upon by others as outsiders. John F. Kennedy would become the first Catholic president of the United States.

PT 20 was a 77-foot Elco boat that won the Plywood Derby.

officers, he realized if he volunteered to serve with PT boats, he could command one right away. It would be a chance to make a difference in the coming war. Commanding a PT boat in the Pacific would be far better than the safe job writing reports that his father had arranged for him at Naval Intelligence in Washington, DC.

The U.S. Navy's focus on motor torpedo boats came from U.S. Army general Douglas MacArthur. The general was stationed in the Philippines and charged with defending the islands from an expected Japanese invasion. Unfortunately, he had very few warships assigned to help him. MacArthur believed that hundreds of small motor torpedo boats would deter an enemy navy from attacking the islands until the U.S. Navy arrived in full force. He requested two hundred PT boats be constructed and sent to his command. But time was running out as the threat of war approached.

When the Japanese invaded the Philippines on December 8, 1941, General MacArthur had only six PT boats under his command. In three months, the American-Filipino forces was trapped and under siege on the Bataan Peninsula west

★ WORLD WAR II ★ *Facts and Trivia*

TORBERT HART MACDONALD

Torbert Hart Macdonald was Jack Kennedy's Harvard roommate and captain of Harvard's varsity football team. He would also become a naval lieutenant and command several PT boats in Squadron 12, stationed in Papua New Guinea, later winning a Silver Star for his heroism. He would go on to serve in Congress and Jack would be a godparent to his son Torbert Macdonald Jr.

JOHN FITZGERALD KENNEDY
Born May 29, 1917, in Brookline, Massachusetts. Prepared at The Choate School. Home Address; 294 Pondfield Road, Bronxville, New York. Winthrop House. *Crimson* (2–4); Chairman Smoker Committee (1); St. Paul's Catholic Club (1–4). Football (1), Junior Varsity (2); Swimming (1), Squad (2). Golf (1). House Hockey (3, 4); House Swimming (2); House Softball (4). Hasty Pudding-Institute of 1770; Spee Club. Permanent Class Committee. Field of Concentration: Government. Intended Vocation: Law.

General Douglas MacArthur photographed in Manila in 1945.

of Manila, where they were cut off from receiving Allied help. When President Franklin D. Roosevelt ordered the general to evacuate the Philippines, MacArthur, his family, and a select few officers boarded the last four PT boats on March 11, 1942, for a 560-mile ocean voyage through enemy-controlled seas to the island of Mindanao. There the party was picked up by American B-17 bombers and flown to Australia.

Lieutenant John Bulkeley commanded the PT boats that led MacArthur to safety. When they had reached Mindanao, MacArthur told him, "You've taken me out of the jaws of death, and I won't forget it." When Lieutenant Bulkeley returned to the United States, he received the Medal of Honor from the president. Later, he would tour the United States recruiting young officers for duty with the newly formed PT squadrons. One of those recruited officers would be the young John F. Kennedy.

Lieutenant Commander John D. Bulkeley receives the Medal of Honor from President Franklin D. Roosevelt in July 1942.

THE PLYWOOD DERBY

The navy began to take a serious look at the different motor torpedo boats that the Europeans had been developing since the end of World War I. At the top of those designs was a seventy-foot wooden speedboat constructed in England by Hubert Scott-Paine in 1938. Named the PV 70, it was powered by three Rolls-Royce Merlin engines that were originally designed for use in aircraft. It was the first boat of that size to sustain forty knots in the rough English Channel.

Henry Sutphen, an American boat builder from the Elco Boat Works, was so impressed with Scott-Paine's design that he purchased the boat and brought it back to the United States. He hoped to demonstrate the boat's qualities and jumpstart an American PT boat program for the U.S. Navy. It was renamed PT 9 and the navy ordered Elco to build eleven more as test boats.

PT boats filled an important need in World War II in shallow waters, complementing the achievements of greater ships in greater seas. This need for small, fast, versatile, strongly armed vessels does not wane.

—John F. Kennedy, 1962

The navy then conducted a test of ten comparative PT boat designs by different boat builders off New London, Connecticut, in July 1941. The winning design would earn a contract from the navy to produce the first American PT boats. The climax of this test was an open-sea race of 190 miles. The course ran from New York Harbor, around the eastern end of Block Island, then around the Fire Island Lightship station, and finished at Montauk Point at the eastern tip of Long Island. Since nearly all the boats were made of wood, the competition became known as the Plywood Derby.

It was a close race. PT 20, an Elco design with a reinforced hull, was the winner. Yet the navy saw merit in all four competing boat designs, and awarded contracts to each of the four companies, with Elco receiving the lion's share of orders to build eighty-foot PT boats.

PT boats under construction at the Elco factory in New Jersey.

Boat builders were required to adopt the same Packard engines. The navy would then add the final touches. It was important that crews had enough room to live on the boat, so the Elco hull design was extended to eighty feet. The extra space also allowed for additional antiaircraft guns on deck. The early class of PT boats were armed with four twenty-one-inch torpedo tubes, a

20mm gun mount, plus two twin-mounted .50-caliber machine guns placed in turrets fore and aft. Depth charge racks were installed on the deck and a smoke screen generator was attached to the stern. Able to attack out of the dark at speeds of over forty knots, launch torpedoes or depth charges, and escape behind smoke screens, the PT boats were a dangerous opponent for enemy ships or submarines.

Among the early orders the navy gave Elco was for an eighty-foot boat numbered PT 109. It was laid down March 4, 1942, by the Elco Works Naval Division in Bayonne, New Jersey. The seventh forty-ton PT boat built in the Bayonne shipyard, PT 109 was launched on June 20, 1942, and delivered to the navy on July 10. On August 20, PT 109 was hoisted aboard the liberty ship USS *Joseph Stanton* to begin its long journey to the war zone in the Pacific and its destiny with Lieutenant John F. Kennedy.

PT 109 waiting for transport to the Pacific aboard the SS Joseph Stanton *on August 20, 1942.*

THE ATTACK ON PEARL HARBOR, DECEMBER 7, 1941, "DATE OF INFAMY"

December 7 began like any other Sunday for most Americans. In Hawaii, the U.S. Navy's Pacific fleet was at anchor in Pearl Harbor. At 7:48 a.m., 360 Japanese aircraft, launched from six aircraft carriers, descended from the skies in a surprise attack. 2,403 Americans were killed, and nearly 1,200 were wounded. Most of the fleet's battleships were heavily damaged or destroyed, including the USS *Arizona*. The attack was planned by Japanese admiral Isoroku Yamamoto, who commanded the Imperial Japanese Navy.

Jack Kennedy was playing football with a friend near the Washington Monument that day. Washington was five hours ahead of Hawaii's time. It was 12:48 p.m. As they drove back from their game, news of the attack came over the radio on CBS: "The Japanese have attacked Pearl Harbor by air, President Roosevelt has just announced."

The following day President Roosevelt asked for and received a Declaration of War from Congress against Japan. The vote for war was 82–0 in the Senate and 388–1 in the House. December 7, Roosevelt proclaimed, would remain "a date which will live in infamy." Four days later, on December 11, Hitler declared Germany was at war with the United States. Italy's dictator, Benito Mussolini, also declared war on the United States that same day. World War II was now a truly global contest.

With confidence in our armed forces, with the unbounding determination of our people, we will gain the inevitable triumph, so help us God.

—President Franklin D. Roosevelt

NAVY
Uncle Sam is calling YO
ENLIST in the Navy
Recruiting Statio
“I WANT YOU IN THE NAV
and I WANT YOU NOW”

CHAPTER 2

A YOUNG VOLUNTEER

*Ask not what your country
can do for you—ask what you
can do for your country.*

—John F. Kennedy

SEPTEMBER 1942, NORTHWESTERN UNIVERSITY, CHICAGO, ILLINOIS, 4:00 P.M.

Jack sat among the officer candidates from his midshipmen class to hear an important guest speaker. Unlike the other students, Jack already held the rank of ensign. He was there because he was tired of the office job the navy had assigned him to in Washington, DC. Jack's father, Joe Kennedy, had pulled strings to get him that job because Jack suffered from a terrible back condition and stomach pains that would have kept him out of military service. But Jack wanted to lead men into action to serve his country in combat against the enemy—not sit at a desk and write reports. So he volunteered for duty at sea and the navy sent him to the Naval Reserve Midshipmen's School at Northwestern University in Chicago to complete his training.

Lieutenant Commander John D. Bulkeley.

Joseph P. Kennedy, United States Ambassador to the United Kingdom

Joseph P. Kennedy was a brilliant and hardworking man. After graduating from Harvard in 1912, he became the youngest bank manager in America. When the United States entered World War I in 1917, Joseph was asked to manage a huge shipbuilding yard in Quincy, Massachusetts.

In Quincy, Joseph became friends with the assistant secretary of the navy, Franklin Delano Roosevelt, who would later become president of the United States in 1933. After amassing a fortune on Wall Street, and supporting Roosevelt's political career, Joseph was asked by President Roosevelt to be the ambassador to Britain in 1938. He served as ambassador until November 1940. It was his dream that his four sons would follow his example and enter politics to serve the American people.

The guest speaker that Kennedy was listening to so avidly that day was Lieutenant Commander John Bulkeley, the commanding officer of Motor Torpedo Boat Squadron 3. Bulkeley was famous for rescuing General MacArthur and his family from the island fortress of Corregidor in Manila Bay, just before the Japanese forced its surrender earlier that year. The Medal of Honor, awarded by President Roosevelt, hung at the collar of Bulkeley's spotless uniform.

Bulkeley was there to recruit officers for action with the patrol boat squadrons. "The PT boat is a great weapon," he proclaimed. "The enemy has not yet won a brush with one. Our little half squadron sank one [Japanese] cruiser, one plane tender, and one loaded transport, badly damaged another cruiser, set a tanker on fire, and shot down four planes." Only later would Jack realize that Bulkeley was telling tall tales.

Appealing to the young men's sense of patriotism and courage, he dared them to volunteer: "Those of you who want to come back after the war and raise families need not apply. PT boat skippers are not coming back!" When Bulkeley asked for twenty volunteers, every man in the room—over a thousand of them—volunteered on the spot. Jack was among the twenty-two chosen.

An aide to Bulkeley recalled the young John F. Kennedy: "He was selling himself hard and expressed a great desire to get in close combat with the enemy as soon as possible . . . he was an intercollegiate sailing champion, had graduated from Harvard with honors and made a favorable impression with . . . his appearance and personality." Jack's intelligence and experience with small boats made him an ideal candidate to command a PT boat. He was ordered upon graduation from junior officer training at Northwestern to the new Motor Torpedo Boat Squadrons Training Center at Melville, Rhode Island.

Quonset (steel) huts at the training center at Melville, 1942.

WHO WERE THE AXIS AND THE ALLIES IN WORLD WAR II?

When Germany invaded Poland on September 1, 1939, an alliance of nations, the Allies, swore to oppose the military aggression of the Axis powers. Initially, the Axis powers in World War II were Germany, Italy, and Japan. On September 27, 1940, they signed a political and military partnership, the Tripartite Pact, opposed to Western democracies and communist countries. Four other nations joined as affiliate states: Bulgaria, Hungary, Romania, and Thailand. Finland also fought on the Axis side until 1944.

Many nations would join the Allies during the war, but there were four principal members: the United Kingdom, the United States, the Soviet Union, and China. These major economic and military powers were known as "The Big Four." Twenty-seven additional countries would join the Allies by 1945.

Victory at all costs, victory in spite of all terror, victory however long and hard the road may be; for without victory, there is no survival.

—Winston Churchill, British Prime Minister

John F. Kennedy (second from right) with his graduating class at Melville in November 1942. Note the PT boat "Mosquito Fleet" emblem on the left.

The training at Melville lasted eight weeks and covered boat handling, engine maintenance, navigation, communications, torpedoes, and tactics. It did not, however, include any training for night maneuvers or rescue. Jack's performance at the school was first rate. He was promoted to lieutenant junior grade when he finished the course in late November.

The Navy then ordered Jack to remain at Melville as an instructor of boat handling, where he was given command of PT 101. This was a great disappointment to Jack. He did not wish to train other men to be PT officers. Jack wished, above all, to be sent into action against the enemy. He would continue to work hard to get his chance.

★ WORLD WAR II ★
Facts and Trivia

THE MOSQUITO FLEET

American PT boats were nicknamed the "Mosquito Fleet" because they were the smallest warships in the navy, and they operated in squadrons. Yet they packed a big sting carrying four torpedoes, and could sink almost any warship. They proved to be the most valuable boats for all kinds of tasks including reconnaissance (searching for the enemy), transporting key people (such as General MacArthur), and rescue operations.

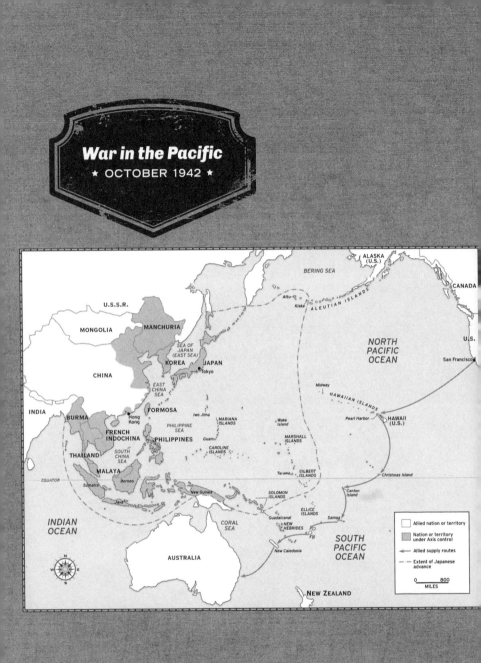

War in the Pacific
★ OCTOBER 1942 ★

ALASKA (U.S.)

BERING SEA

CANADA

U.S.S.R.

MONGOLIA

MANCHURIA

ALEUTIAN ISLANDS

Attu
Kiska

NORTH PACIFIC OCEAN

U.S.

SEA OF JAPAN (EAST SEA)

KOREA   JAPAN
Tokyo

San Francisco

CHINA

EAST CHINA SEA

FORMOSA

Midway

HAWAIIAN ISLANDS

INDIA

BURMA   Hong Kong

Iwo Jima

MARIANA ISLANDS

Wake Island

Pearl Harbor   HAWAII (U.S.)

PHILIPPINE SEA

FRENCH INDOCHINA

PHILIPPINES   Guam

CAROLINE ISLANDS

MARSHALL ISLANDS

THAILAND

SOUTH CHINA SEA

MALAYA

Sumatra   Borneo

EQUATOR

Tarawa   GILBERT ISLANDS

Christmas Island

Java

New Guinea

SOLOMON ISLANDS

Canton Island

INDIAN OCEAN

CORAL SEA

Guadalcanal   ELLICE ISLANDS

NEW HEBRIDES   Samoa

Fiji

SOUTH PACIFIC OCEAN

AUSTRALIA

New Caledonia

NEW ZEALAND

N
W   E
S

	Allied nation or territory
	Nation or territory under Axis control
	Allied supply routes
	Extent of Japanese advance

0   800
MILES

CHAPTER 3

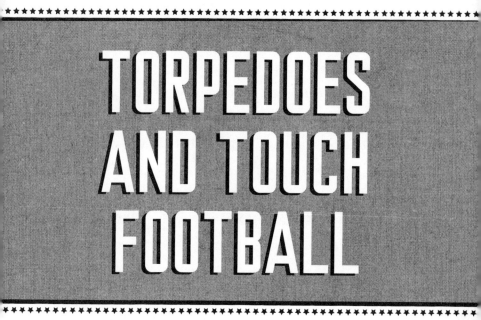

TORPEDOES AND TOUCH FOOTBALL

*A war is not won if the defeated enemy
has not been turned into a friend.*

—Eric Hoffer

DECEMBER 2, 1942, PT TRAINING BASE, MELVILLE, RHODE ISLAND, 2:30 P.M.

Ensign Paul Burgess "Red" Fay had just arrived at Melville
for PT boat training. A number of the new students were

outside playing touch football before classes started the next day. "The game was only under way for about half an hour," Fay recalled, "when a seemingly young, bright-looking, skinny boy with a sweater turned inside out with an *H* sewed on the inside asked if he could get in the game. 'Get another man and you're in!' I replied. In about ten minutes this young fellow was back with another player—who looked like he had a lot more potential.

"Two plays hadn't been run before this skinny boy stopped play with a claim that we were not adhering to the rules . . . I protested loudly, but the other players, including some of those on my team, agreed with the skinny kid." Fay announced to his teammates that he would cover the new kid. "In the plays that followed," Fay recalled, "I saw nothing but elbows, shoulders, and knees, and acquired a collection of bumps and bruises."

George "Barney" Ross, also new to Melville, was on Jack's team. "I thought he was maybe seventeen or eighteen years old, and I thought he was a young enlisted man . . . ," Barney remembered. "And he had a letter sweater with an *H* on his back . . . he seemed to be running the team." Barney thought the kid was doing all right. He wondered if he had just graduated from a boarding school he knew near Princeton. Barney asked, "Are you from the Hun School?" The skinny kid replied, "No, I'm from Harvard."

Jack Kennedy and Paul "Red" Fay in 1943.

The skinny kid helped his team trounce Fay and his friends. Unable to keep up with the nimble newcomer, Fay's teammates kept asking him, "Who's got the skinny kid?" Fay was angry. Who was this skinny guy in the college sweater?

The next day they learned the "skinny guy" was Lieutenant John F. Kennedy, their commanding officer and instructor on PT 101. Fay was still nursing a grudge because his team had lost to Kennedy's at football. He refused to board PT 101 and held up a class from the day's training while he joined a different boat.

PT 117 under way in early 1943. PT 117 was an 80-foot Elco and a sister ship to PT 109.

When they returned from their exercise, Jack called Fay into his office and cut him down to size, threatening to expel him from the school. "Do you realize," Jack scolded Fay, "that if everybody did what you did today, the Japanese would be marching in Times Square at Christmastime?" Fay realized he was out of line and begged for a second chance. In the weeks that followed, the rival players became good friends.

Within months, almost everyone at Melville received orders to report to active torpedo boat squadrons. Barney Ross and Paul Fay received orders to report to Motor Torpedo Boat Squadron 10, which was fighting in the Solomon Islands in the Pacific. Jack Kennedy, however, was not among those with orders to head for war.

Jack remained at Melville, Rhode Island, as an instructor. He soon received orders to join Torpedo Boat Squadron 14 and was deployed to Central America to help defend the Panama Canal. Sitting out the war in this new assignment was still not what Jack had in mind: He wanted to be at the frontlines of battle. Jack's older brother, Joe Jr., had been assigned to San Juan, Puerto Rico, to fly search missions for German submarines in a sector where no submarines had ever been seen. The brothers realized their powerful father had probably pulled strings again to keep them out of any real danger.

The Kennedy brothers were determined to bypass their father and get into the war. Joe Jr. volunteered for the war in Europe, while Jack applied for a combat assignment in the

★ WORLD WAR II ★
Facts and Trivia

PAUL BURGESS "RED" FAY JR.

Paul Burgess "Red" Fay Jr. would be a lifelong friend of Jack Kennedy and would help him win all his elections to the U.S. House of Representatives, the U.S. Senate, and finally his campaign to become the U.S. president in 1961. The day he was sworn in as president, Jack appointed Fay as undersecretary of the navy.

Lieutenant John F. Kennedy and Ensign Joseph P. Kennedy Jr. in May 1942.

Pacific. He asked for help from Massachusetts senator David Walsh, chairman of the Senate Naval Affairs Committee, whom he had met several months earlier through family connections. Luckily for Jack, his efforts were soon rewarded.

Jack wrote a friend, "Having reached my limit—several months before the definitive word on Panama came down from on high—I immediately appealed directly to various wise men (skipping father) and also filled out the official form for change-of-assignment. The distinguished Senator Walsh shortly responded by obtaining some beautiful words on navy department letter head that order me to the Solomon

Islands: Motor Torpedo Boat Squadron 2."

On March 15, 1943, Jack boarded the USS *Rochambeau,*
a converted ocean liner bound for the New Hebrides in the
South Pacific. From there he would transfer to a smaller
ship, a landing ship tank (LST) that would carry him to his
destiny in the Solomon Islands with PT 109. He took with
him a small collection of his favorite books, a record player,
and a good-luck gold coin given to him by Mrs. Clare Luce,
a friend of the Kennedy family. The coin had belonged to
her mother. Jack attached the coin to his navy "dog tags"
(metal identity tags worn around a sailor's neck) before he
left home and wrote his thanks to Mrs. Luce. Finally, Jack
was headed to war.

The USS Rochambeau.

Solomon Islanders in a handmade wooden dugout canoe.

PART TWO

Combat in the Solomon Islands

*I wish I could tell you about the South Pacific.
The way it actually was. The endless ocean.
The infinite specks of coral we called islands.
Coconut palms nodding gracefully toward
the ocean. Reefs upon which waves broke
into spray, and inner lagoons, lovely beyond
description. I wish I could tell you about the
sweating jungle, the full moon rising behind
the volcanoes, and the waiting. The waiting.
The timeless, repetitive waiting.*

—James A. Michener, *Tales of the South Pacific*

Lieutenant John F. Kennedy in 1942 before shipping out for the Solomons.

CHAPTER 4

INTO THE BREACH

Cry "Havoc," and let
slip the dogs of war.

—William Shakespeare, *Julius Caesar*

OFF THE COAST OF GUADALCANAL, SOLOMON ISLANDS, APRIL 7, 1943

Jack was reading in his bunk on board LST 449 as it neared the Solomon Islands. Abruptly, the ship listed to one side and then the other as it began a zigzag course. Jack leaped from his bunk and moved toward the deck above to see what was happening. He heard the sound of the ship's guns firing. Suddenly, the ship heaved upward, rocked by explosions. Running onto the deck, Jack looked skyward. They were under attack by at least nine enemy planes.

★ **47** ★

A Japanese bomber had narrowly missed the ship with a five-hundred-pound bomb off the starboard bow. A second near miss landed near the port bow, and three more fell close to the starboard side, damaging the LST. The explosions threw up gigantic geysers of water, drenching the ship. They had been extremely lucky. The LST was loaded with a cargo of munitions. One single direct hit would have killed them all.

Jack ran to the nearest gun position to help pass ammunition to the crew. Everyone was scared. One of those crewmen, a kid from South Dakota named Ted Guthrie, remembered, "I was only sixteen years old and scared to death, our ship had just been straddled by bombs, and our gun tub was knee deep in water. I wanted to run, but gained strength from the courage shown by Mr. Kennedy."

Next to LST 449 was the escorting destroyer USS *Aaron Ward*. It was struck by two bombs and several near misses, which caused severe flooding. Twenty-seven men were killed and many were wounded. Other ships began to tow the stricken vessel toward shore to prevent it from sinking. As the *Aaron Ward* limped away, Jack saw the tanker USS *Kanawha* in the distance take a direct hit and explode in flames. The *Aaron Ward* sank shortly after, just six hundred yards from shore.

As the attack ended, a Japanese pilot floated down on a parachute into the water nearby. The captain of Jack's ship obeyed the law of the sea, which expected sailors to help one another—even enemy sailors, if they needed rescue. However, as the Americans moved closer to the Japanese airman, he drew a pistol and began firing at his rescuers. They had no choice but to shoot him where he floated.

The enemy's courage impressed Jack. He wrote his best friend, Lem Billings, "I had been praising the Lord and passing the ammunition right alongside—but that slowed me a bit—the thought of him sitting in the water battling an entire ship . . . it brought home very strongly how long it is going to take to finish this war."

★ WORLD WAR II ★ *Facts and Trivia*

WHY DID THE JAPANESE FIGHT TO THE DEATH?

The Japanese believed their emperor, Hirohito, was a living god. Children were taught from an early age to honor their family and their emperor. Somewhat akin to chivalrous European knights, Japanese military men followed a strict code of behavior based on an age-old way of life called *Bushido*, which means "way of the warrior." Samurai warriors followed this code, which dictated it was the soldier's highest honor to fight and, if necessary, die for the emperor. According to *Bushido*, a soldier was forbidden to surrender or to be captured. If this happened, then it would bring extreme shame to the soldier and to his entire family. Since the military ruled wartime Japan, this belief system was constantly reinforced to everyone.

Jack Kennedy at the helm of PT 109 in the Solomon Islands, 1943.

CHAPTER 5

A DANGEROUS PARADISE

The South Pacific is memorable because when you are in the islands you simply cannot ignore nature. You cannot avoid looking up at the stars, large as apples on a new tree. You cannot deafen your ear to the thunder of the surf. The bright sands, the screaming birds, and the wild winds are always with you.

—James A. Michener, *Return to Paradise*

The Solomons were the perfect image of what Americans envisioned the equatorial South Pacific would be like. Active volcanoes rose out of the sea on islands covered in palm trees and tropical flowers. The ocean was a crystal-clear azure blue filled with dolphins and sea turtles, and Islanders fishing from small dugout canoes. The sun-drenched islands were a picture-perfect, sandy beach paradise to the unwary traveler.

Beneath the vision of paradise, however, dangers lurked at every step. The islands were a sea of mud, rotting vegetation, and dense swamps where mosquitoes and flies bred in the millions. Tropical diseases were rampant—malaria, dengue and yellow fever, dysentery and typhoid, to name a few—all potentially lethal.

In the ocean among the uncharted reefs and sandbars, man-eating white-tip sharks patrolled along with salt-water crocodiles and huge meat-eating barracuda fish. The fast-flowing currents and waves could easily sweep people away from land and out to sea. Razor-sharp coral surrounded each island just below the surface of the water, beyond which the ocean depth fell away to an abyss of a thousand feet or more.

The sun beat down every day in relentless, merciless heat. When it rained, which almost every day, the islands were lashed by tropical downpours. Everything remained

THE SOLOMON ISLANDS

The war in the Solomon Islands was at the edge of the known world. Lying off the eastern shore of Papua New Guinea, the Solomons are a parallel chain of small islands stretching for six hundred miles from Buka and Bougainville, just below the equator, to San Cristobal to the southeast. When the Spanish navigator Álvaro de Mendaña de Neira first visited them in 1568, he thought he'd discovered gold, so he christened them the "Islands of Solomon" after the wealthy biblical king.

In 1893, the British arrived and declared the Solomons under the protection of their empire. They quickly established several coconut plantations and missionary churches throughout the archipelago, with a governor's mansion on the island of Tulagi. The Islanders, a collection of Melanesian tribes, were mostly converted to Christianity by the time of World War II.

Lieutenant Ted Robinson, who served with Jack in Tulagi, said of the Melanesians, "Their major diet was fish, coconuts, and tara, a kind of potato, that they grew in their gardens . . . The Solomon Islands were owned by the British and the natives spoke a form of pidgin English that we could understand . . . and malaria and dengue fever was prevalent."

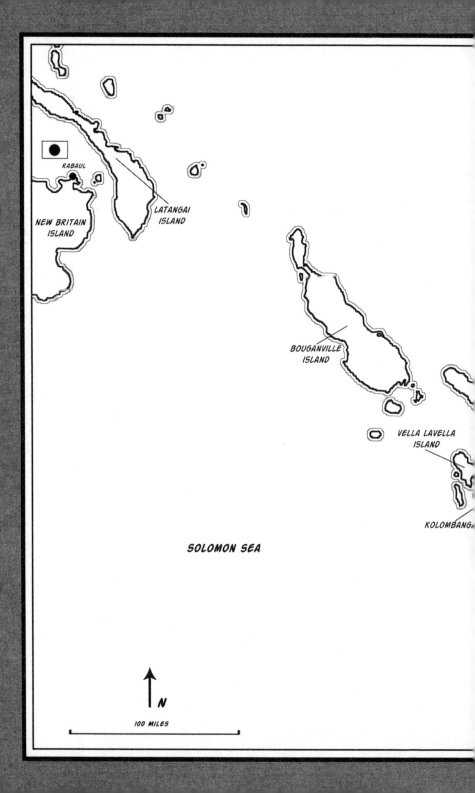

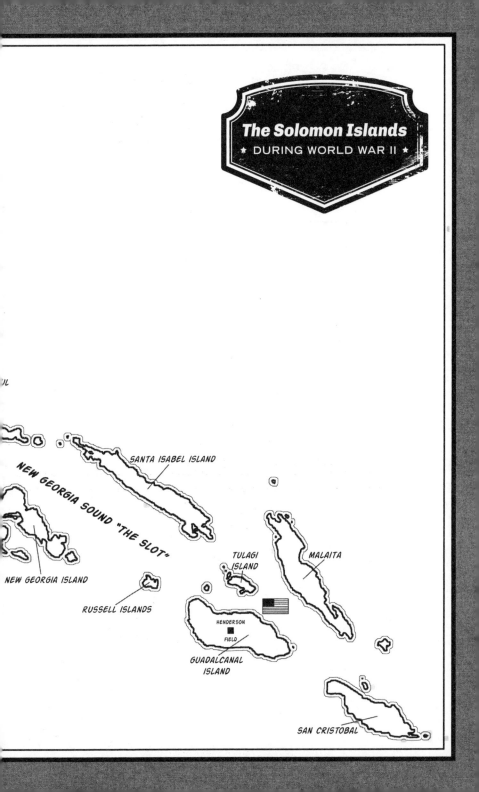

That bubble I had about lying on a cool Pacific island . . . is definitely a bubble that has burst. You can't even swim, there is some sort of fungus in the water that grows out of your ears, which will be all I need . . .

—Jack in a letter to a friend, April 1943

WAR REPORT

JAPAN'S CONQUEST OF THE PACIFIC REGION 1941–1942

Japan is an island nation with few natural resources. The Japanese government, under Prime Minister Hideki Tojo, already fighting a major war in China, launched an all-out war against the United States and Great Britain in December of 1941, in a carefully timed assault to capture the natural resources of the Pacific. Japan wanted to create a self-sustaining colonial empire, free of their American and European rivals. In the opening months of the war, Japan seized a vast area of islands and lands that were former European colonial possessions as well as the Philippines, a group of Pacific islands under the protection of the United States.

hot, humid, and moldy. Under such conditions, food spoiled instantly, equipment rusted, and clothes disintegrated as people fell prey to infections and disease.

Jack London, the famous American writer and adventurer, visited the Solomons in 1908 and nearly died of fever. He wrote a friend, "If I were a King, the worst punishment I could inflict on my enemies would be to banish them to the Solomons. On second thought: King or no King, I don't think I'd have the heart to do it!"

Yet it was the Solomons, this ancient collection of little islands, that became the battleground between the Allies and the Empire of Japan. It was here where the fate of nations hung in the balance as two great navies battled for control of the sea and their armies fought for the islands. Caught in between were the Melanesian Islanders, who called World War II "the big death."

PT 109 under the command of Ensign Bryant L. Larson, arriving at Tulagi on the morning of December 1, 1942, after the Battle of Tassafaronga.

CHAPTER 6

THE PT 109

Oh, some PTs do seventy-five,
And some do sixty-nine;
When we get ours to run at all
We think we're doing fine . . .

—PT boat crew song

PT BOAT BASE AT TULAGI,
SOLOMON ISLANDS, APRIL 25, 1943

Jack arrived in the Solomons to command PT 109 as a replacement skipper. By that time, PT 109 was a veteran boat. It had been in service since November 1942, completing twenty-two patrols under two previous skippers. It had already been in six combat actions, including the rescue of ninety-four survivors from the sunken heavy cruiser USS *Northampton* on December 1, 1942. Jack's crew was new to

PT 109, except its executive officer, Ensign Leonard J. Thom. The veteran sailors they replaced had either been transferred to other assignments or had returned to the United States.

The boat was a mess. The tropical climate, the months of hard service, and the salt water had taken their toll. The hull was covered with barnacles and green slime below the waterline. It needed to be stripped and repainted, the engines needed overhauling, the weapons needed servicing, and the supplies needed to be restocked.

Worst of all, the boat stank to high heaven. It had been hidden for a time under the trees in a swamp on Florida Island without a crew. The crew cabins were crawling with bugs, mice, and rats. There was even a rotting fish below deck where a bird had dropped it. The crew had a

PT boats in floating dry docks at the Rendova Motor Torpedo Boat Base, Central Solomons.

The official U.S. Navy model of PT 109. Note the life raft lashed to the forward deck that was later removed to install a 37mm antitank gun.

lot of hard work ahead to prepare the boat for action.

When Jack arrived, all the sailors working on the PT 109 deck set aside their tools, mops, and paintbrushes to salute their new lieutenant. Rumors had been flying among the enlisted men, for some time, that Jack Kennedy was an Ivy League rich kid, the son of the former ambassador to Britain, Joseph Kennedy from Boston. Surely, he would not make much of a leader. And there he was, twenty-five years old, rather thin, with a mop of brown hair. Radioman John Maguire admitted to a friend, "Geez, I don't know if I want to go out with this guy. He looks fifteen."

But much to the men's surprise, their new lieutenant, "Mr. Kennedy," as they referred to him, took off his shirt and got right to work alongside them. As an officer, he was not expected to do that, but Jack earned their respect by

THE PT 109 CREW ON AUGUST 2, 1943

LT. (JG) John F. Kennedy Commanding Officer

ENSIGN Leonard J. Thom Executive Officer

ENSIGN George "Barney" H. R. Ross Lookout/Gunner

S1C Edman Edgar Mauer Quartermaster/Cook/Signalman

RM2C John E. Maguire Radioman

S1C Raymond Albert Gunner

GM2C Charles A. Harris Gunner

MOMM1C Gerard E. Zinser Motor Mechanic

MOMM1C Patrick H. McMahon Motor Mechanic

MOMM2C Harold W. Marney Gunner

MOMM2C William Johnston Gunner

TM2C Raymond L. Starkey Torpedoman

TM2C Andrew J. Kirksey Torpedoman

helping out. Over the next several weeks, the crew worked hard to get PT 109 ready for its next mission at sea. When they were done, PT 109 was painted with a dark-green camouflage so it would be hard to see under the palm trees or out on the sea at night.

From then on, Jack began to earn his reputation as a good leader. He was easy to talk to and he didn't make much of his rich family background or officer status. The men liked him. Torpedoman Raymond Starkey said that Jack "was all business, but with a sense of humor and modest and considerate of enlisted men." Jack would often trade with other ships for ice cream and candy for the men—hard-to-come-by treats in the Solomon Islands. The men understood that "Mr. Kennedy" took care of his crew.

His boat was shipshape and his crew was well organized, orderly. He was twenty-five—he was an old man—the rest of us were a bunch of kids.
—Ensign John "Johnny" Iles, Skipper of PT 48 and PT 105

Maurice Kowal, one of the original PT 109 crewmen who was later transferred, said, "He was terrific, he was a good man. He took care of us all the time. He would go over to Guadalcanal and bum supplies, particularly ice cream. He was crazy for ice cream."

The navy set up two PT boat outposts near Guadalcanal in August 1942. The main PT boat base on Tulagi Island was at the village of Sesapi, where the PT squadrons had a command center and a floating dry dock to repair the boats. A second base was set up at another small village across the channel on Florida Island. This was named Calvertville by the sailors after the first officer to take charge of the new base. It was at this new, secret base that the PT squadrons would live and work by day while hiding their boats close to shore (even in the swamps), and then operating against the Japanese at night. Adopting the well-built Islander huts,

Calvertville was a Tulagi PT boat base named for Commander Allen P. Calvert, who commanded Motor Torpedo Boat Squadron 1 in the Solomons in 1942.

Calvertville quickly became a mix of Melanesian culture and American technology.

An American officer who served with Jack admired the Islanders' way of life. "I found, throughout the tropics, the army and marines usually followed the practice of cutting down every tree in sight, then putting up hot canvas tents and wondering why their men all suffered from heatstroke. We, however, discovered that the local Melanesian natives knew how to live in the tropics. Tulagi was ten degrees south of the equator and you can't get much hotter than that. They always placed their villages on a fresh water stream overlooking a protected bay under a heavy cover of palm trees where there was a prevailing breeze off the water. Then they built thatched roof huts, with air space under the floor and open sides, so the breeze could flow under and through the hut."

Little did Jack know that trading with the locals and learning some of their pidgin English (a mix of Melanesian and English words both cultures could easily understand) would soon be critical to saving his life and the lives of his PT 109 crew. A friend of Jack's serving on PT boats said of the Islanders, "They were a gentle people, very loyal to the British crown and would risk their lives to save us." Jack would soon discover just how true his friend's words would prove to be.

PT 105, a sister ship of PT 109, during training exercises in July 1942.

CHAPTER 7

TRAINING FOR WAR

*You can only fight
the way you practice.*

—Miyamoto Musashi, *A Book of Five Rings*

By the time Jack took command of PT 109, the Japanese and the Allies were in a relatively quiet period between major battles. The Japanese had evacuated Guadalcanal in February and retreated to the island of New Georgia two hundred miles to the northwest. The next Allied advance would begin in June. This gave Jack and his crew a few precious weeks to train and run night patrols around Tulagi, where enemy ships were no longer seen.

★ **67** ★

"On good nights it's beautiful," Jack wrote home, "the water is amazingly phosphorescent, flying fishes which shine like lights are zooming around, and you usually get two or three porpoises who lodge right under the bow, and no matter how fast the boat goes keep just about six inches ahead of the boat."

Jack got to know his crew. He already knew his executive officer, Leonard "Lennie" Thom, from PT training at Melville. Thom was a former Ohio State University football star, over six feet tall and two hundred and twenty pounds, with blond hair and a beard. People joked that he looked like a modern-day Viking. Jack wrote home that when the next big move against the Japanese came, they would be well-protected because of Ensign Thom.

The others in the crew were mostly green and inexperienced sailors, and like Jack, new to the war. They practiced working as a team taking the boat to sea, going to battle stations, making practice torpedo runs, and shooting the machine guns at oil barrels floating on the water. In war, every second counts and can mean the difference between life and death. Jack pushed the training hard, writing his parents, "I'd like to be confident they know the difference between firing a gun and winding their watch . . ." Luckily, PT 109 had an excellent crew.

Three of the men were from Jack's home state of

Massachusetts: Charles "Bucky" Harris, Maurice Kowal, and William Johnston. This trio was younger than their new skipper. At twenty-five, Andrew Kirksey was the same age as Jack, but he was already married with a son. The rest of the men were older: John Maguire was twenty-six; Edman Mauer, who went by Edgar, was twenty-eight; and Edmund Drewitch and Leon Drawdy were both thirty.

Finally, there was the old man of the boat, the "only enlisted seaman I feel I have to call 'sir,'" Jack said, and that was Patrick "Pop" McMahon, forty-one, who was the boat's chief engineer. The men worked on the boat during the day, then caught a few hours of sleep and went on patrol at night. They usually slept on the deck when not on patrol, to stay as cool as possible in the tropical heat.

Food was bad, mostly canned C-rations (cold prepackaged meals), SPAM (a canned precooked meat), beans, and stew. The biggest treat everyone craved was an ice cream made from powder. When it could be obtained, they would mix up a batch and store it in their small refrigerators on the boats.

Cold drinks and ice cream were the only luxuries the navy men had to look forward to in the war zone, so refrigerators were an important piece of equipment on the PT boats. When one of the boats in Squadron 5 (PT boats were organized into groups of up to twelve boats called squadrons) took damage from enemy fire that destroyed its refrigerator, all the other boats promptly installed armor plate behind each of theirs to protect them from a similar fate.

For entertainment, the men played cards, wrote letters home, and listened to music and news provided by an enemy radio show called "Zero Hour" that was hosted by an English-speaking woman known as "Tokyo Rose." Jack had brought a Victrola record player with him from home. He had a small collection of popular songs and Broadway show tunes that he played for the men. But the song he listened to over and over again was a song from the 1941 Broadway show *Lady in the Dark*, entitled "My Ship." The lyrics were by the famous American composer Ira Gershwin.

MY SHIP

My ship has sails that are made of silk,
The decks are trimmed with gold,
And of jam and spice, there's a paradise
in the hold.
My ship's aglow with a million pearls
And rubies fill each bin,
The sun sits high in a sapphire sky
When my ship comes in.

The only enemy they encountered in the first few weeks at Tulagi was the nightly Japanese visitor "Washing

WHO WAS TOKYO ROSE?

Tokyo Rose was the nickname for an English-speaking woman who broadcast radio programs from Japan, filled with anti-American news and popular American music. The broadcasts were meant to hurt the Allies' morale and inspire fear. Tokyo Rose could often name the Allied units and their movements with accuracy. Yet it was all great entertainment for the American servicemen, and "she" was wildly popular.

In fact, Tokyo Rose was not one woman, but actually a number of different English-speaking women. The one who was most remembered was Iva Toguri D'Aquino from Los Angeles. She had been in Japan, visiting her family, when war broke out. The Japanese government forced her to make these radio broadcasts as one of the women nicknamed Tokyo Rose.

Even though Toguri refused to broadcast anti-American statements and even risked her life to smuggle food to Allied prisoners of war, she was convicted of treason when she tried to return to the United States in 1947 and received a ten-year sentence. President Ford granted her a pardon in 1977.

Machine Charlie," a lone aircraft that arrived in darkness and dropped a few bombs. This potentially lethal greeting forced everyone to get up and dive for cover. The real goal of such raids, however, was to wake everyone up and keep them on edge. The tactic worked, and the Americans had no way of stopping the raiders from coming. Jack thought it was safer to be out on patrol at night than sitting ducks waiting for enemy bombs.

On May 30, PT 109 and several other boats were ordered to move to the Russell Islands, thirty miles northwest of Tulagi and closer to the Japanese base on New Georgia (which was the next target for Allied invasion). The two islands that made up the Russells had been occupied by the Japanese in 1942, but the enemy decided to pull back to positions at Munda, on the island of New Georgia, over 120 miles farther to the northwest. Although the Japanese were not far away, their ships no longer ventured as far south as the Russells.

The time in the Russells was a chance for Jack to continue training the crew on night patrols around the islands. It was here that Jack earned one of his several nicknames. Since the PT boats operated at night, one of the major jobs was to fuel the boats the next day. The gasoline was stored in huge oil drums stockpiled at the base. As it was a small outfit, the

THE NEW GEORGIA SOUND—"THE SLOT"

Allied naval commanders referred to the New Georgia Sound, the body of water running through the middle of the Solomon Islands, as "The Slot." It was through this channel that the Japanese would send warships and supply convoys to their embattled soldiers on Guadalcanal and New Georgia. There were so many Japanese and Allied ships sunk during naval clashes in the waters north of Guadalcanal that the area was renamed "Iron Bottom Sound."

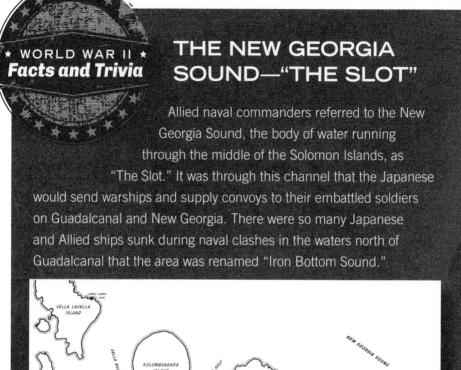

base in the Russells had no fuel tanks or machine pumps. So, the refueling had to be done with hand pumps, emptying fifty-four-gallon oil drums to fill the boat's three-thousand-gallon tanks. The operation took many hours to complete.

PT boat crews quickly figured out that the first boat in from patrol would be the first one to refuel at the only gas station at the base. The winning crew, therefore, would be able to sleep a few more hours than everyone else before the next mission. It soon became a race between boats to be the first one home after each mission. Jack's chief engineer, Pat McMahon, warned him the PT 109's engines were likely to give him trouble if he tried to throw them into reverse suddenly. In spite of the warning, Jack didn't listen.

On a race home, Jack had the engines wide open, going as fast as the boat could carry them. When they approached the fuel depot at the pier, he ordered McMahon to throw the engines into reverse to slow the boat. Just as McMahon had warned would happen, the engines stalled, and PT 109 sailed right into the pier. Men and tools went flying. A few sailors had to leap off the pier to avoid the crash. Many swore at Jack for his careless mistake. For a while afterward they all called the skipper "Crash Kennedy."

Luckily, Jack was on good terms with his commanding officer, who laughed off the serious incident. A friend of Jack's explained, "we were all young wild things, and if we were lucky enough to live through a night patrol many of us raced our boats in—happy to be alive . . . A little frolicking was understood and forgiven."

After two weeks of training missions, PT 109 and several other boats were moved again on June 16 to a tiny mudflat of an island called Lumbari, off the northern tip of Rendova Island and just south across the channel from the main Japanese positions on New Georgia. Until the Allies landed on New Georgia a month later, on July 13, to capture the Japanese airfield at Munda, Jack's new home was the most forward Allied position in the Solomons.

Conditions at Lumbari were very basic. Unlike the luxurious base at Calvertville or the comfortable plantation house in the Russells, there were no huts to sleep in, no showers or mess hall. The base was just a few tents, a command bunker, and slit trenches half filled with water. Because of the mud-flats offshore, the boats had to be moored in the open, where they were exposed to air attack. The only reliable food was C-rations. The place was seething with flies and mosquitoes.

Lumbari had one redeeming feature—it was close to the enemy, whose main outpost was just across the channel at Munda. If you were a PT skipper looking to go hunting for enemy shipping, this was where you wanted to be. The PT boats were ordered to attack any Japanese supply missions sent down The Slot to their positions on New Georgia. The happy training days were over; the PT squadrons were going into harm's way.

A PT boat traveling at high speed, leaving a large wake behind it.

CHAPTER 8

INTO THE UNKNOWN

*Courage is resistance to fear, mastery
of fear, not absence of fear.*

—Mark Twain

JULY 19, 1943, VELLA GULF NORTH OF GIZO ISLAND, CLOSE TO MIDNIGHT

It was PT 109's first patrol into Vella Gulf, far into enemy-held territory. Though the night was dark, Leon Drawdy saw a plane flying toward them at under a hundred feet. It was so close, he could even make out the Japanese rising sun on each of its wings. He shouted a warning, but two bombs

hit close to PT 109 before anyone could react. The boat was
rocked by the explosions as red-hot metal fragments sprayed
across the deck and into the hull.

"This work, once dull, has suddenly turned deadly . . . ,"
Jack wrote home a few days later. "We were well up in
there—lying to thinking this wasn't too tough, when suddenly I heard a plane and looked up . . . The next minute I
was flat on my back across the deck. He had straddled us
with a couple of bombs."

Jack described what it was like to be under an air attack.
"They usually drop a flare—of terrific brilliance—everything stands out for what seems miles around—you wait
then as you can't see a thing up in the air—the next minute
there's a heck of a craaack—they have dropped one or two
bombs. All in all, it makes for a certain loss of appetite."

The boat was full of holes. It had been a close call. Two
crewmen, Maurice Kowal and Leon Drawdy, were injured
by the attack. They would both leave for medical treatment
and not return to PT 109. Edmund Drewitch would also leave
the boat due to a minor injury. They were replaced by three
newcomers on loan from Torpedo Squadron 10: torpedoman's

mate Raymond L. Starkey, from Garden Grove, California, aged twenty-nine; machinist's mate Harold William Marney, from Springfield, Massachusetts, aged nineteen; and motor mechanic Gerard E. Zinser from Belleville, Illinois, aged twenty-five.

Torpedoman Andrew Kirksey was terrified by what had nearly happened. He began to envision his own death, saying to friends, "I won't be around much longer." Yet he never asked to be relieved of duty. Jack decided he would allow him to transfer to shore duty the next time they were back at the Tulagi base. He wrote home, "When a fellow gets the feeling that he's in for it—the only thing to do is let him get off the boat—because strangely enough they always seem to be the ones that do get it."

★ WORLD WAR II ★
Facts and Trivia

A PHOSPHORESCENT WAKE?

When a ship moves through water, it creates waves as the ship's propellers churn the water behind the stern. These effects are known as a ship's wake. In the tropics, the seas are filled with tiny living organisms called plankton, which glow in the dark when disturbed. While traveling at speed, PT boats created a huge wake, easily visible at night. From the air looking down, Japanese pilots could see a boat's wake as the churned-up water glowed in the dark, pointing directly toward its creator. Enemy bombers used this effect to target American PT boats at night and were the main threat American sailors faced in the Solomons.

The Japanese used air power to support their surface ships as part of the Tokyo Express, bringing troops and supplies into the Solomon Islands.

CHAPTER 9

THE TOKYO EXPRESS

When the enemy is relaxed, make them toil.
When full, starve them. When settled, make
them move.

—Sun Tzu, *The Art of War*

PT BOAT BASE, RENDOVA ISLAND, AUGUST 1, 1943, 3:00 P.M.

Jack was meeting with other officers in their tent when the air raid sirens blared the alarm. Seconds later, eighteen Japanese planes bore down on the small base in a surprise raid. Jack dove into a foxhole for cover and then raced toward PT 109 tied up near shore.

"Cast off!" Jack yelled as he leaped aboard.

Enemy bombs and torpedoes rained down on the assembled boats as they scrambled for open water. A bomb hit PT 164, destroying the boat and killing two of her crew. The boat's torpedoes launched from their wrecked tubes and careened around the harbor, adding to the deadly chaos. PT 117 was also hit by an enemy bomb and completely destroyed. Flames, smoke, and wreckage crowded the harbor as PT 109 and the other boats raced out to sea to escape the trap.

When the attack ended, the skippers assembled at their headquarters' tent. Commander Thomas Warfield held a secret message from the American admiralty. The Japanese were sending a supply convoy down The Slot that night to resupply their base at Kolombangara. These ships would not be the usual slow-moving barges. The enemy was sending the "Tokyo Express" of fast-moving destroyers. Admiral Halsey was sending a flotilla of American destroyers to try to intercept them. Warfield ordered his PT boats to get ready: "We've got to use everything we have." All available PT boats would be heading out that night to try to hit the enemy convoy if the enemy ships got past Halsey's destroyers.

It was going to be a moonless night with lots of cloud

cover. Conditions were perfect for the enemy ships to reach Kolombangara without being seen. Only four of the PT boats were equipped with radar, so they would lead the others to the enemy. The PT boats were organized into four groups that would fight independently. Each group had four PT boats, led by the one equipped with radar. Boats were ordered to stay close to one another in the dark and maintain radio silence. They would be operating far into enemy-held territory.

Commander Thomas G. Warfield briefing his PT boat captains before they leave for a night mission in the Solomons.

Jack ran into Ensign Barney Ross on his way back to PT 109 from the command post. They were friends from their training days together at Melville. Ten days earlier Barney's PT 166 had been destroyed and he was not yet assigned to another boat. Hearing of the biggest PT mission ever planned for that night, Ross wanted to be in on the action.

"Do you mind if I come along, Jack?" Ross asked.

"No, come on," said Jack, "I'm short of men anyway."

When they reached the boat, Jack told the crew the bad news.

"We are going out tonight," Jack told the men. "Let's get ready."

The new mission meant a change of orders for PT 109. Jack's boat had originally been left off the duty schedule that night. The crew was exhausted from operating all week and had been looking forward to a rest. No one was happy to be heading into a fight with the enemy. And more bad news—Jack had brought Ensign Barney Ross along for this mission. The crew had nothing against Ross personally, but it was an old sailor's superstition that a stranger aboard a ship brought bad luck.

On the forward deck of PT 109, the crew had lashed down an army 37mm antitank gun. This was an experiment ordered by the navy to try to improve the PT boat's firepower against enemy barges. In the makeshift attempt to secure the gun, its wheels had been removed and the axle was held fast by lashing it to two large wooden planks measuring two feet wide and eight feet long. To make room for the new weapon, the life raft that was usually stored on the forward deck was removed.

Ensign Ross would serve as the forward gunner and lookout. A few of the men noted that with the addition of Ensign Ross to the boat, the number of crewmen was now thirteen—an unlucky number. Once again, Andrew Kirksey's fears took hold of him. He told the others, "I won't be going home." Kirksey's hands shook so badly, he had to put down his cup of coffee. When offered the chance to sit out that night's mission, he refused. Kirksey would stay at his post and do his duty.

★ WORLD WAR II ★
Facts and Trivia

WHAT WAS THE TOKYO EXPRESS?

The Tokyo Express was an Allied phrase to describe the nighttime Japanese reinforcement and supply missions to the Solomon Islands. When the Allies began flying warplanes from Henderson Field on Guadalcanal, it became too dangerous for the enemy to use slow-moving freighters and transports for these missions. Instead, the Japanese began using fast-moving destroyers to move troops and supplies to their forward positions in the Solomons. Only destroyers had the speed required to be out of Allied air range by daylight. Since they only ran these missions at night, the Japanese referred to them as "Rat Transportation."

John F. Kennedy (left), George "Barney" Ross (rear), and
Paul "Red" Fay (right) in August 1943.

PART THREE

Survival

To live is to suffer, to survive is to find

some meaning in the suffering.

—Friedrich Nietzsche

An illustration by Tom Freeman that shows the fateful PT 109 collision with a Japanese destroyer.

THE DARK VALLEY

Even though I walk through the valley
of the shadow of death,

I will fear no evil, for you are with me;

your rod and your staff, they comfort me.

—Psalm 23:4

BLACKETT STRAIT, EAST OF GIZO ISLAND, AUGUST 2, 1943, 2:27 A.M.

Jack stood at the wheel of PT 109, staring into the night. "It was as dark as if you were in a closet with the door shut,"

Ensign Ross remembered, "it was that kind of night, no moon, no stars." In the humid air, a heavy mist rose above the ocean. It was nearly impossible to see anything, but Jack and his twelve-man crew remained alert. They were all prepared for battle, wearing steel helmets and life vests. Somewhere out there in the blackness, they knew enemy ships were coming. Their only chance against an enemy warship was to remain hidden in the night in order to deliver a surprise torpedo attack.

In the darkness, the lead boat in Kennedy's group became separated, leaving the others without radar. PT 109 crept forward at four knots, searching for the enemy. Running only on the centerline engine to reduce their visible wake, the crew listened for the approach of a ship or the drone of an enemy aircraft diving to attack them. PT 162 and PT 169 patrolled just behind and to the right as Jack led the formation eastward. Not one of the three boats was equipped with radar that would have allowed them to see what lay ahead in the black night.

Suddenly, from the southeast near the shore of Kolombangara Island, came flashes of light and the sound of big guns firing while flares and searchlights probed the night's inky darkness—*THUMP! THUMP! CRACK! BOOM!* A battle was under way as American PT boats engaged the enemy, but no one in Jack's group could see what was

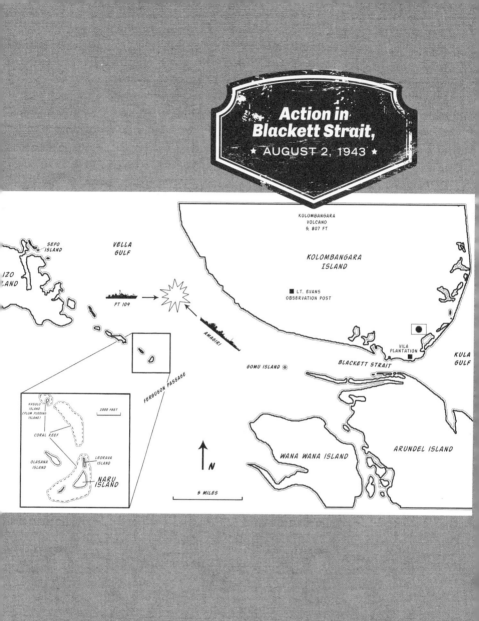

Action in Blackett Strait, ★ AUGUST 2, 1943 ★

SEPO ISLAND

VELLA GULF

IZO AND

PT 109

KOLOMBANGARA VOLCANO 5, 807 FT

KOLOMBANGARA ISLAND

LT. EVANS OBSERVATION POST

AMAGIRI

VILA PLANTATION

KULA GULF

GOMU ISLAND

BLACKETT STRAIT

FERGUSON PASSAGE

KASOLO ISLAND (PLUM PUDDING ISLAND)

2000 FEET

CORAL REEF

OLASANA ISLAND

LEORAVA ISLAND

NARU ISLAND

WANA WANA ISLAND

ARUNDEL ISLAND

N

5 MILES

happening. Below deck in the cabin, the radio bellowed frantic signals from other American boats as they broke radio silence.

"I have fired torpedoes! I am under heavy fire from enemy destroyers! I am under heavy fire! Shells all around me!"

"Get out of there, you're in a trap, you're in a trap! Get out!"

* *

"Ship at two o'clock!" Harold Marney hollered from PT 109's forward gun turret. All hands looked to the right. Less than a thousand yards away, the telltale bow wave of another ship approached through the blackness, and it was moving fast. With the high mountain on Kolombangara behind it, the approaching vessel was nearly invisible except for its wake. The ship was forty seconds away . . .

"Lenny, look at this!" Jack shouted to Ensign Thom.

At first Jack thought it must be another American patrol boat, but the oncoming ship was massive. Then, as they watched, it began turning right for them. It was a Japanese destroyer!

"Sound general quarters!" yelled Jack to Maguire. Thirty seconds . . .

"GENERAL QUARTERS!" hollered Maguire toward the rear of the boat, where the crew who were not on watch scrambled for their battle stations. On the bow, Ensign Ross fumbled to load a 37mm shell into their new weapon. Jack jammed the lever on his dashboard to signal Pop McMahon in the engine room below that he needed emergency power from all three engines as Maguire turned the arming key for the torpedo tubes. Twenty seconds . . .

Jack spun the wheel to starboard, desperately trying to steer the boat away from the onrushing tower of steel. If he could turn the boat, Jack hoped to try to fire his torpedoes, even though the range was closing fast. With only the centerline engine in gear, the boat responded sluggishly, unable to gain speed or maneuver. He waited for the dashboard indicator to register that all engines were in gear as precious seconds ticked by. The bow wave of the enemy ship drew nearer, white water against the blackness of the sea. Ten seconds . . .

Jack threw the throttles forward, and the boat began to surge ahead. Loaded with fuel, weapons, and ammunition, the boat weighed nearly fifty tons and could not simply speed away. PT 109 moved forward at an angle to the oncoming ship, now towering over them, but it was already too late. There was nothing anyone could do. Several of Kennedy's crew leaped over the side to avoid certain death. Maguire grabbed the rosary around his neck and prayed. One second . . .

The steel bow of the destroyer smashed into the wooden hull of PT 109 with tremendous force, reducing the boat to kindling, and it kept on going, splitting the boat diagonally across its beam, slicing off a section of the stern. Jack was thrown hard against the controls and onto the deck, injuring his back. Looking up, as the steel hull of the enemy ship tore through what remained of his boat, a single thought crossed his mind: *So this is what it's like to die.*

Instantly there was a roar as bright flames shot hundreds of feet skyward when gasoline from PT 109's ruptured fuel tanks ignited. Intent on escaping and trailing fire on its hull, the Japanese ship raced off into the night, leaving the sea covered with wreckage, gasoline, flames, and stunned men. The forward half of PT 109 remained, half-sunk and down by the stern where the starboard engine had been sheared away, lit up by fires all around on the surface of the sea.

Below in the engine room, McMahon was engulfed in flames that had exploded into his compartment from the hatch to the next room. He held his breath and threw his hands in front of his face to try to protect himself—but there was no escape. Then, just as suddenly, the deck beneath his feet was crushed and sucked below the black water, and he was gone.

Nearby, Lieutenant Phil Potter, the skipper of PT 169, saw the explosion, covered his face with his hands, and sobbed,

"My God! My God!" His crew looked away. Their friends were dead; no one could have survived such an explosion. Potter's crew tried to fire two torpedoes at the enemy destroyer but both failed to launch from their tubes. PT 169 retreated at high speed to escape the now-alerted enemy.

Lieutenant John Lowrey, commanding PT 162 next to Jack's boat, was also completely rattled by the shock of what happened. Lawrence Ogilvie, a crewman on PT 162,

Jack Kirksey, whose father served alongside Kennedy on PT 109, visits PT 617, a restored 80-foot Elco PT boat at the National PT Boat Museum in Fall River, MA, in June 2017.

THE JAPANESE DESTROYER *AMAGIRI*

The *Amagiri* "Heavenly Mist" was a Fubuki-class destroyer launched on February 27, 1930, at the Ishikawajima Shipyards in Tokyo, Japan. The 388-foot destroyer was capable of making thirty-eight knots and was heavily armed with six five-inch guns, nine torpedo tubes, thirty-six depth charges, and thirty-two antiaircraft guns. She survived the Solomons campaign only to be sunk by a mine on April 23, 1944, in Makassar Strait, between the islands of Borneo to the west and Sulawesi to the east (both islands are now part of Indonesia).

recalled, "We were about 200 to 250 feet apart, and it was so dark, we could only see the wake of the boat ahead of us. I was on watch at the port .50 caliber gun tub looking through binoculars and couldn't see a thing, until the 109 was hit . . . We were stunned and never fired a shot, trying to realize what had happened. We didn't think anyone from the crew could live through that and Lieutenant Lowrey took us out of there."

Lieutenant Potter later claimed that a search was conducted, but Jack and his surviving crew would not be found that night. There is no record that Lieutenant Lowrey made a search. Lieutenant Richard Keresey, who commanded PT 105, stated years later, "The tragedy was that the comrades of the 109 did not go back to look for survivors, even though we saw the search as hopeless. We had not yet learned that hopeless searches should still be made, so that those of us who still had to go out night after night would know that, if we did not return, our comrades would look for us and would fight to save us beyond any reasonable expectation. We should have gone back."

Australian Coastwatcher Lieutenant Arthur Reginald Evans.

CHAPTER 11

THE COAST-WATCHER

One person can make a difference,
and everyone should try.

—John F. Kennedy

SECRET ALLIED OBSERVATION POST, KOLOMBANGARA ISLAND, AUGUST 2, 1943, 2:30 A.M.

High up on the volcanic mountainside of Kolombangara, Royal Australian naval lieutenant Arthur Reginald Evans sat in complete darkness atop his lookout post. Of all the

Allied servicemen in the Pacific war, Arthur had perhaps the loneliest and most dangerous job of all. He belonged to the Coastwatchers, an elite group of officers and civilian spies who had knowledge of the Solomon Islands and volunteered to work behind enemy lines to report on enemy movements and activity.

Arthur's post was located 1,400 feet up the side of the ancient volcano in a jungle so dense it was nearly impossible to reach. Friendly Melanesians protected him from discovery by the Japanese. They also carried all his supplies, including the heavy radios used to communicate with Allied headquarters. Without the Islanders' help, no Coastwatcher would survive for long.

On this night, Arthur had witnessed the frantic battle raging up and down Blackett Strait as American PT boats engaged the Tokyo Express. In the last of these skirmishes, there was suddenly a huge fireball and burning fuel on the sea. Evans was sure two ships had collided in the dark—but whose ships were they?

* * *

The destroyed stern of PT 109 was underwater as the bow jutted upward. Watertight compartments within the hull kept the wreck afloat. In places, the sea itself was on fire as spilled gasoline burned. Jack clung to the wrecked bow.

In the chaos and flames on all sides, Jack didn't know if he was alone.

"Who's aboard?!" yelled Jack.

John Maguire, Edgar Mauer, and Raymond Albert answered his call. Jack feared any remaining fuel below deck might explode at any second, killing them all.

"Over the side!" Jack commanded.

The four men leaped into the sea. Swimming near the wreck, Jack noticed the wake of the passing destroyer had luckily pushed the burning gasoline away from PT 109. Since their chances of survival were better if they remained with the boat, he had the group swim back and climbed aboard the half-sunken bow section. Jack hollered for the other missing crewmen. He could hear their cries for help but couldn't see them.

Those who were able answered their skipper's call. Mauer had salvaged one of the ship's battery-operated lanterns. Jack told him to blink the light so the men in the water could find them on the wreck. Jack had a flare gun, but he chose not to use it. If the Japanese saw flares, they would know where to find their helpless vessel.

The ocean currents were already sweeping PT 109 down the channel. Jack knew they had to gather the survivors at the wreck or they might never be found. The men in the water were already widely scattered. Most of them wore life vests, which would keep them afloat for a time.

Johnston hadn't been on watch at the moment of danger and had been dozing on the deck when he heard Maguire yell out the general quarters alarm. When the enemy ship hit them, Johnston was thrown overboard and spun round and round underwater by the movement of the destroyer's propellers—a close brush with certain death. He surfaced in a pool of gasoline that remarkably had not burned. Unable to breathe, he inhaled the toxic fumes, which knocked him unconscious. Only his life vest saved him from drowning.

Starkey was flung onto the stern section of the boat, which quickly sank. Suddenly, he was alone in the water, with his face and hands stinging from flash burns, and he panicked. He was afraid of the Japanese and of the sharks they all knew were in these waters. Starkey thought of his wife and their four-year-old daughter. He knew if he wanted to see them again he needed to pull himself together. Then he saw the wrecked bow section of PT 109 several hundred yards away, and through the shifting darkness he saw the others. He kicked off his shoes and started swimming toward them.

Gerard Zinser had just been relieved of his engine room watch by Pop McMahon. He came up through the engine room hatch onto the deck and heard Marney's warning of a ship approaching. The next thing he knew, his body was tossed through the air and into the sea.

Charles Harris, the gunner's mate, had leaped from the deck to avoid being crushed by the bow of the destroyer. He surfaced far from the burning wreck of PT 109, and feared he was the only survivor. Then, in the light of the fires, he saw a man with his back to him, in a life vest nearby. He was still wearing his helmet, pleading for someone to help take it off. Harris swam to him and carefully pulled away the helmet. It was McMahon, and he was terribly burned.

Harris shouted toward the wreck, "Mr. Kennedy! Mr. Kennedy! McMahon is badly hurt." Jack quickly removed his shirt, shoes, and his .38 revolver and jumped into the dark water, swimming toward the sound of Harris's voice a hundred yards away. He found Harris next to McMahon, helping him as best he could.

"How are you, Mac?" Jack asked when he reached the wounded mechanic.

"I'm all right," McMahon said. "I'm kind of burnt."

Even in the darkness, Jack could tell McMahon was terribly wounded. He had third-degree burns on his face, hands, and arms. He was in shock and terrible pain, and unable to swim. Only his life vest kept his head above water.

"Go on, skipper," the old engineer said to Kennedy. "You go on. I've had it."

Jack would have none of that kind of talk. He took a strap from McMahon's life vest and pulled him back toward the wreck, which was now drifting away from them with the current. As the fires died down, they were enclosed in total darkness. The other men called out their positions, and Jack kept swimming toward them. When the three of them made it back to the boat almost an hour later, they set McMahon down gently on what remained of the listing deck.

Ensign Thom had been thrown from the boat and was knocked out by the impact, but he came to with help from Zinser and Ross, who were floating nearby. Zinser's arms were badly burned. On the wreck, Maguire heard their cries for help and swam out to lead them back. Along the way, Ensign Thom found Johnston floating unconscious in a pool of gasoline. He dragged the gunner back to the wreck by his life vest. Starkey managed to swim back to the wreck on his own.

Jack swam from man to man, checking on their condition. In addition to those suffering from burns, Harris had taken a hard blow to one leg and could barely swim. Several men were unconscious or sick from the gasoline fumes. Harold Marney and Andrew Kirksey were both still missing.

"Marney! Kirksey!" The men yelled into the blackness, hoping to find them. No answer came. They kept calling for thirty minutes. It seemed as though the two sailors had simply disappeared in the collision. The men all hoped their shipmates would appear, but for the moment they had to focus on their own survival.

Harold W. Marney, Machinist's Mate 2nd Class.

Adrift now, forty miles behind enemy lines, without food or fresh drinking water, without a radio or map, and with only a few handguns to defend themselves, Jack and his ten survivors could only hope for rescue before the Japanese found them. They hoped and prayed an American PT boat would arrive to save them before dawn, but none came. They were on their own. Every decision Jack made would mean life or death for them all.

SECRET ALLIED OBSERVATION POST, KOLOMBANGARA ISLAND, AUGUST 2, 1943, 6:35 A.M.

At dawn, Lieutenant Evans looked through his telescope and saw wreckage floating with the current. He radioed Allied headquarters that the enemy ships had retreated to the northwest and that there was wreckage visible in the channel. Within hours a reply came: "PT Boat 109 lost in action in Blackett Strait two miles southwest Meresu Cove. Crew of twelve. Request any information." (Allied command did not know Ensign Ross had joined PT 109 as a last-minute volunteer, making the crew number thirteen.)

Evans replied, "No survivors so far. Object still floating between Meresu and Gizo." Then he put out the word to his scouts on the island to look out for any marooned American sailors. Evans knew if there were survivors, he had to find them before the enemy. It was possible the men could have washed up on one of the islands in Blackett Strait. He would need to send scouts at the first opportunity to search for them.

When the fourteen PT boats of Torpedo Boat Squadron 2

returned to their base at Rendova Island and reported the loss of PT 109, several of Jack's friends wanted to mount a search and rescue mission without delay. But Lieutenant Commander Thomas Warfield refused to allow any of his squadron's boats to make the attempt. The Japanese controlled the air by day, and Kennedy's boat was sunk forty miles *behind* enemy lines.

Lieutenant Phil Potter of PT 169 reported to Lieutenant Commander Warfield on the loss of PT 109 and the gasoline

Andrew Jackson Kirksey.

THE MISSING MEN AND WOMEN OF WORLD WAR II

Of the 16 million Americans who served in World War II, more than 400,000 died during the war. At the end of the war, there were approximately 79,000 Americans unaccounted for. This number included those buried with honor as unknowns, officially buried at sea, lost at sea, and missing in action. Today, more than 73,000 Americans remain unaccounted for from World War II.

IN MEMORY OF
ANDREW J KIRKSEY
TM2
US NAVY
WORLD WAR II
NOV 5 1917
AUG 3 1944
KIA

IN MEMORY OF
HAROLD W MARNEY
MOMM2
US NAVY
WORLD WAR II
OCT 25 1924
AUG 2 1943
KIA

Andrew Kirksey and Harold Marney have memorial markers at the Agawam Veterans Memorial Cemetery in Agawam, MA. They are located in the "In Memory" section, which recognizes veterans who were killed and whose bodies were never recovered.

explosion. He said that PT 169 had made a search of the area in which Jack's boat had collided with the Japanese destroyer. There was no way, Potter believed, that anyone could have survived.

Warfield decided he could not risk losing any more men to search for Jack Kennedy and his crew. Instead, he would report them missing, and ordered their personal belongings be collected and sent home. Telegrams would then be sent to the next of kin, and within a few days, the mothers and fathers or the wives of the missing crew would know their loved ones were missing and probably dead.

Still, some clung to the hope that Jack and his crew were alive and waiting to be rescued. It was decided that an air search of Blackett Strait would be conducted as soon as possible. If anyone was still alive, they would have to locate them soon. The PT boats would not be risked without confirmation of survivors, so all hope rested on a sharp-eyed pilot seeing them from the air. Meanwhile, the war moved relentlessly forward without PT 109 and its crew.

Blackett Strait, where PT 109 was rammed on the night of August 2, 1943. Naru Island is on the right, Olasana is on the left, and the volcano on Kolombangara rises in the distance.

PLUM PUDDING ISLAND

It takes courage to grow up and
become who you really are.

—E. E. Cummings

BLACKETT STRAIT, AUGUST 2, 1943, 6:35 A.M.

When dawn arrived, the survivors of PT 109 could see the huge volcano on Kolombangara to the northeast just a few miles away. The Japanese had ten thousand soldiers there. To the west lay the island of Vella Lavella and to the south, only a mile distant, was the island of Gizo. Jack knew both islands were held by Japanese forces. If the wreck of their boat was spotted by any Japanese lookouts, they would surely be captured.

Jack looked at his crew. They were in a bad way. No one had any food or even a canteen of fresh water to drink. Worse still, the bow of the wreck was gurgling as it slowly filled with water and listed to one side. Soon it would roll over and sink. Jack knew they had to decide what they were going to do next. Time was running out.

If they surrendered to the Japanese, there was no telling what would happen. The enemy's treatment of Allied prisoners was brutal, often fatal. They might refuse to take them prisoner and kill them instead. Yet, if they were taken prisoner, at least there was a chance of survival. If they chose to evade the enemy, they could easily perish at sea without their loved ones ever knowing what became of them. Jack knew some of his men had wives and children. He felt he should let them decide.

"What do you want to do if the [Japanese] come out?" Jack asked the men. "Fight or surrender?"

The men looked at one another. What could they fight with? They were armed with a few waterlogged handguns, one Thompson submachine gun, and some knives. They would not be able to put up much of a struggle if the Japanese arrived. The crew responded together, "Anything you say, Mr. Kennedy. You're the boss."

They waited, still hoping for rescue now that they could be seen in daylight. The sun rose overhead. Around ten o'clock, the wreck gurgled and sighed and turned turtle. The men clung to the sides of the upside-down hull. Johnston, who was delirious, and the badly burned McMahon were laid down on the overturned hull and held in place by their friends.

No American boats had come to find them. No Allied search planes were seen overhead. By midday, Jack had to make the tough decision. He knew the wreck would soon be underwater, and they had to try to reach land before darkness fell. It was time to swim for their lives. Jack's years on the Harvard swim team and his survival training from the navy were about to pay off.

Jack pointed to one of the smaller islands in the channel to the southwest. It was a tiny speck of sand nicknamed Plum Pudding Island by the British colonials for its shape. The Melanesians called it Kasolo Island. "We will swim to that small island. We have less chance of making it than some of these other islands here, but there'll be less chance of Japanese too."

It was going to be a long swim, over three miles away, but the ocean current was with them. The hard part was keeping everyone together. Not all the men were good swimmers, some were injured, and all were exhausted.

Jack organized the men into two groups. The best swimmers would help pull those too weak to swim on one of the two large wooden timbers they salvaged from the wreck—the same timber they had used to lash down the 37mm gun. Ensign Thom would lead them. McMahon was too badly burned to hang on to a makeshift raft. He rested on what remained of the upturned hull. Jack swam over to him.

"Mac, you and I will go together."

"I'll just keep you back," McMahon replied. "You go on with the other men—don't worry about me." But Jack wouldn't let him give up.

"What in the hell are you talking about?" Jack said. "Get your butt in the water!"

Cutting a strap from McMahon's life vest, Jack used it as a rope to tow the wounded sailor. He swam a breaststroke as McMahon floated on his back. When Jack's arms became tired, he put the strap between his teeth to keep going. Every so often he would check how McMahon was holding up. The mechanic was in a lot of pain with the salt water licking his terrible burns, but he did not complain.

"How do you feel, Mac?" Jack said.

"How far do we have to go?" McMahon asked.

"We are doing good," Jack assured him.

As the hours dragged by, McMahon's strength began to fail; the pain was too much.

John F. Kennedy swimming for Harvard during his senior year, 1938.

"Skip, I'm all done. I can't make it," he told Jack. "Leave me here."

"Whether you like it or not, you're coming, Pappy," Jack said. "Don't you know only the good die young?"

It took them four hours to swim the three and a half miles to Plum Pudding Island. It was just a hundred yards long and forty yards wide, a speck of sand with a few coconut trees. When Jack and McMahon reached the beach, Jack, exhausted from his ordeal, vomited seawater he had

Plum Pudding Island, later renamed Kennedy Island, photographed in 2002.

swallowed. Knowing they would be helpless if the enemy saw them out in the open, McMahon struggled to his feet and with his burned arms helped Jack crawl up the sand and into cover. To their great fortune, there were no Japanese on the island.

The other men reached shore and huddled among the trees to stay out of sight. Just as they got under cover, a Japanese barge chugged its way past the island. No one moved and the enemy ship disappeared up the channel. Everyone lay on the sand, dead tired. If the enemy had appeared moments earlier, all of them would have been caught helpless in the open water.

I served twenty years in the navy, and I never had an officer that would ever come close to what I saw Kennedy do.
—Motor Mechanic First Class Gerard E. Zinser

Jack knew the small group of palm trees provided only an illusion of safety. They remained well behind enemy lines, with precious little cover to hide in. There was no fresh water on this island and no food other than a few coconuts. They had not seen an Allied boat or aircraft all day.

The skipper knew that if his men were to be rescued, something had to be done, and it was his duty to save them. Unbeknownst to Jack, his instincts were correct. The aircraft sent to look for survivors arrived too late in the day and found wreckage but no survivors. There would be no further attempt to rescue the men. They were completely on their own.

Islands from bottom to top: Naru, Olasana, and Gizo. Kasolo (Plum Pudding Island) is out of sight at the top right. Note the coral reefs extending from Naru, which Jack Kennedy and George Ross crossed to reach Ferguson Passage, the deep water below Naru Island.

CHAPTER 13

ADRIFT AT SEA

*There is no greater love than to lay
down one's life for one's friends.*

—John 15:13

PLUM PUDDING ISLAND, BLACKETT STRAIT, AUGUST 2, 1943, 6:30 P.M.

Jack was worn out, sick to his stomach, and aching from his strained back. Nevertheless, he knew his crew was just as sick and bone tired as he was. McMahon's wounds were going to kill him if he didn't get help soon. These men's lives now rested in Jack's hands—he was their skipper. Jack got them into this mess, and he would do his utmost to get them out of it. He knew their best chance of rescue would be in the first twenty-four hours. Soon, an idea formed in his mind.

Ferguson Passage was just beyond Naru Island to the south, a mile and a half distant from Plum Pudding Island. Jack knew American PT boats had patrolled there for the past several nights. A series of reefs that surrounded the islands would allow him to walk much of the way over the coral in shallow water. If he could reach Ferguson Passage and swim out with the lantern, he might be able to signal a boat and lead it back to pick up his crew. It was a desperate and dangerous plan, but Jack saw no alternative. If he did nothing, they would all start dying in a matter of days—if the enemy didn't finish them off first.

Jack threw on a life vest, tied his .38 revolver around his neck with a cord, put on a pair of shoes to protect his feet against the coral, and grabbed the lantern wrapped in a life vest. When he told the others of his plan, they tried to stop him, but he was determined to make the effort.

Jack left instructions. "If I find a boat, I'll flash the lantern twice. The password will be *Roger*, the answer will be *Wilco*." Ensign Thom was left in charge. The men would stand watches through the night to look for his signal or the approach of danger. Jack shook hands with Thom before walking out into the ocean. Jack made his way to the reef on which he could stand and wade in chest-deep water toward Naru Island and Ferguson Passage beyond. In between sections of reef, he had to swim, dragging the heavy lantern with him.

Along the way, Jack took note of the landmarks so he could find his way back. It was almost dark by the time he made it to the edge of the reef surrounding Naru Island. As he waded through the waves he saw the shadow of an enormous fish. Was it a shark? He flashed the lantern and splashed water hard to try to scare it away. The shadow vanished. *Would it return? Were there others?*

Before him to the south, as far as he could see, was Ferguson Passage. With any luck, American PT boats would return to patrol there within hours. Jack took off his shoes, tied them to his waist, and took a deep breath. He was a single man at the edge of night. Stepping off the coral ledge, he swam far out into the open waters of the channel. He held the lantern close to his chest and strained to listen for the throb of engines or the sight of flares. If he saw a boat, he planned to fire his revolver into the air and flash the lantern to signal for help.

For the first time in his life, Jack was truly alone. Half a world away from his father, all the money and power he had grown up with could not help him now. His fate was in the hands of nature.

Hours later, a few lights appeared far to the west, many miles distant. Jack realized the PT boats were not coming through the channel that night and began the long swim back to his men. He made it to the reef but could not summon the energy to climb out of the water as the ocean currents swept him away. The changing current pushed Jack farther away from Plum Pudding Island. He flashed his lantern and hollered, "Roger! Roger!" Jack was desperate for his friends to hear him and come to his aid. He didn't have the strength to try to swim for shore, so he surrendered to the current.

The men thought they saw a flash of light and raced into the surf. Did they hear Jack calling to them from the dark? Was the light they saw Jack's lantern or a reflection off the water? Had Jack been swept past and out to sea? Standing on the coral reef, they tried to locate him in the black of night, but Jack did not appear. Their moment of joy at the thought of rescue was replaced with a feeling of doom. Their leader was gone. Someone said, "We are going to die."

Johnston would have none of it. "Aw, shut up. You can't die. Only the good die young."

FERGUSON PASSAGE, AUGUST 3, 1943, IN THE DARK HOURS BEFORE DAWN

Jack was beyond exhaustion. He stopped trying to swim, letting the currents take him where they would. In a desperate effort to stay afloat, he let go of his shoes. Yet he clung to the lantern, still wrapped in a life vest. It was his only way to signal his friends. Perhaps it was his way to keep hope alive—there might yet be a way out of this.

The temperature at night had dropped, and Jack was very cold. His mind was in a daze as the ocean swept him along. Home was a long, long way off. Time no longer had any meaning. Held up by the life vest, he moved with the sea's currents. In the darkness, he could not make out any of the islands he knew were close by. Jack knew he was drifting northward and he feared washing ashore on Kolombangara, where he would surely be captured by the Japanese.

A small miracle saved him. Before dawn, the tides changed and the currents reversed to the southeast and back into Ferguson Passage. By dawn, Jack could make out his surroundings and realized he was close to where he had started his swim the night before. Nature had given him a second chance to try to make it back to his men.

Jack struck out for Plum Pudding Island a second time. Fearing he would drown from fatigue, he swam first to Leorava Island, the closest land just north of Naru. Leorava was just a stretch of sand above the waves, but it would allow him to rest. As he struggled to make it to the beach, the surrounding reef of razor-sharp coral sliced open his bare feet and legs. When he reached the sand, he collapsed and fell into a deep sleep.

Hours later he awoke and tried the lantern. It no longer

worked, so he left it. Using his last ounce of energy, he began to make his way back to Plum Pudding Island, stumbling over rocks, climbing along the reef in chest-deep water, and swimming the deep channels toward his men, who must have given him up for dead. Since the collision, he had been in the water for over thirty hours. With no food or fresh water to drink, and suffering badly from the bruises and cuts inflicted by scraping against the coral, it took the deepest reserves of will to keep himself going.

> To me the sea is a continual miracle, / The fishes that swim—the rocks—the motion of the waves—the ships with men in them, / What stranger miracles are there?
> —Walt Whitman

Unknown to the survivors of PT 109, the Japanese used the cover of that moonless night to land hundreds of soldiers on the island of Gizo, west across the channel from Plum Pudding Island. Two Melanesian scouts loyal to the Allied Coastwatchers witnessed the enemy landings from their post on the nearby island of Sepo. They knew this important information must reach the Coastwatchers through their leader, Lieutenant Arthur Evans. In the early morning of

August 3, as Jack was making his way back to Plum Pudding Island, the scouts boarded their dugout canoe and made for the island of Kolombangara to speak to Evans.

Their names were Biuku Gasa and Eroni Kumana, both nineteen years old and best friends. They were native Melanesians who had received a brief education from Methodist teachers. They spoke only a few words of English, but they understood the Japanese were no friends of the Islanders. They were fiercely loyal to the Allies, and

Islander scouts Biuku Gasa (left) and Eroni Kumana, photographed in 1962.

especially to Lieutenant Evans. They would travel two days in their canoe and risk their lives to bring Evans the news of the enemy landings on Gizo.

• •

Back on Plum Pudding Island, the men took stock of their situation. It was hard not to despair. Johnston was semiconscious after swallowing gasoline the night before. Harris could hardly stand on his badly swollen leg, injured during the collision. Zinser had second-degree burns on his arms. But no one was worse off than Pop McMahon, who sat in terrible pain and misery. The third-degree burns on his face, upper body, and hands had swollen. The crew's medical kit had been lost with the boat, so there was very little the men could do for him.

Kennedy had not returned. It was nearing midday and he had been gone since dusk the night before. The men assumed he had been swept away in the ocean currents and lost at sea. Or maybe the Japanese had captured him. Of course, there was always the chance he had been attacked by a shark. They feared the worst and their hopes sank. Jack Kennedy had been a terrific skipper.

All the men were weary from the swim and their injuries, hungry and burning with thirst. No one had eaten in two days. Above them in the trees were a few coconuts. Mauer decided to climb a tree to knock some down. On the way up, he was bitten on his leg by red ants and tumbled back down in a hurry to brush them off. On his second try he reached the top and tossed down three coconuts. When he got back to the ground, Mauer struggled to open them with his knife.

When coconuts are ripe, they hold a small amount of fresh water that is safe to drink. When Mauer opened the coconuts, he took the first drink and then helped McMahon, sitting next to him. The others passed around their first meal, drinking the warm water and eating the fruit inside. On the sand, they saw land crabs that inhabit the Solomons moving along over the beach and the jungle floor, where everyone rested. No one moved to try to catch one. They were all hungry, but not *that* hungry. Not yet, anyway.

Suddenly, Maguire saw something out in the surf. A man was swimming toward them! "Here's Kirksey!" he shouted to the others. But it was not the long-lost Kirksey—Jack had finally returned. Ross and Thom ran from the trees to help their leader from the water. Ross tried to help him to his feet, but Jack fell into the sand, vomiting seawater and gasping for air. They carried him under the cover of the trees. Jack was suffering from the early stages of hypothermia and he was shaking uncontrollably. Leonard Thom gave him a great bear hug until he warmed up.

Once he was able to speak, Jack explained that he had

not seen any boats and had been swept away by the current. Then he collapsed into a deep sleep. Later he awoke briefly and looked up at Ensign Ross. He managed to tell him, "Ross, you try tonight," before returning to his deep slumber.

• •

Ensign Ross was afraid of what Jack had ordered him to do. He was not as strong a swimmer as Jack, nor as confident he would find his way back. Jack warned him to be at the edge of Ferguson Passage before dark to be sure of his location. The thought of leaving the group to swim out alone into the unknown was terrifying, but he knew there was a chance that if American boats were in the channel that night he might signal a rescue. Without the lantern, however, the only way to signal a boat was with Jack's revolver. Though Ross was afraid, he obeyed his skipper's orders.

Ross knew the sun set quickly in the tropics, just after 6:30 p.m., so he began his trek to the edge of Ferguson Passage at 4:00 that afternoon, picking his way across the reef. As Jack had advised him, Ross noted the landmarks nearby to ensure he would find his way back to Plum Pudding the next morning. By dusk, he stood in chest-deep water on the last reef before the deep channel, where they hoped the American boats would patrol again. As darkness fell, the sight of land plummeted, and soon he stood in complete darkness. The sound of the wind and the waves was his only company. Feeling hopeless, Ross still made the swim into Fergusson Passage, trying to keep his bearings. Taking Jack's revolver tied around his neck, he fired a shot into the air. *BAM!* The blast from the gun was lost in the vast blackness around him. He would later fire a second and a third signal before giving up and making his way back to the reef. Following Jack's course, he stumbled and swam to Leorava Island, where he rested until daylight. When he could see where he was, Ross made his way back across the reef to Plum Pudding Island.

● ●

LIEUTENANT ARTHUR EVANS'S HIDEOUT, KOLOMBANGARA ISLAND, WEDNESDAY, AUGUST 4, 8:00 A.M.

Biuku and Eroni, the local scouts, arrived at Lieutenant Evans's hideout after stopping overnight on the island of Wana Wana. They reported the Japanese had landed hundreds of soldiers on the island of Gizo two nights before. It was critical information, and Evans was glad they had come to see him. But Evans had an even more important question for the young scouts.

"Have you seen any shipwrecked survivors on Gizo?"

Biuku Gasa in 1943.

he asked. They said they had seen a huge fiery explosion at sea a few nights ago, but they couldn't tell what had happened. They had not seen any survivors. Evans told them the Americans had lost a patrol boat in Blackett Strait two nights ago, and there might be shipwrecked survivors on the islands around Gizo. They were ordered to look for them. Biuku and Eroni agreed and made their way back to their canoe for the long trip back to Sepo Island.

The standing orders for all Melanesian scouts were to bring any downed aviators, either Allied or Japanese, back to Evans. They would be rewarded for each rescue with canned food, weapons and ammunition, or other trade goods. To help them identify Americans (who were new to the Islanders since the Solomons were ruled by the British before the war), they were taught that Americans flew aircraft with big white stars on the wings. The scouts knew if any such people were found, it was their duty to help them in any way possible. Biuku and Eroni understood they had now been entrusted with a special mission—to search for and rescue any American survivors.

Kennedy and the PT 109 survivors kept themselves alive by eating coconuts from trees like this one.

CHAPTER 14

SCOUTING OLASANA ISLAND

Nature is indifferent to the survival of the human species, including Americans.

—Adlai E. Stevenson

When Ross got back to Plum Pudding Island, everyone was glad he was all right, but distressed that he hadn't seen any boats. Even though Johnston was feeling better and Jack had revived after his long sleep, the spirits of the men worsened. They complained openly that the navy had let them down, saying, "Where are the boats, anyway?" All except for Jack, who would not show his own fears in front of his crew. He made jokes to lighten their mood. "What I would give for a can of grapefruit juice!" he told Zinser.

Jack remained convinced their best hope of rescue was to signal an American boat in Ferguson Passage. Sooner or later the PT boats would return to these waters. He also knew they could not stay on Plum Pudding Island. There was no fresh water and there were too few trees for them to only eat coconuts. Thirst was now their greatest enemy. Jack knew they absolutely had to find fresh water. The time had come to make one of those decisions that might get them all killed or captured, or that could lead them back to safety.

A mile and a half from Plum Pudding Island to the southwest was Olasana Island, next to Naru Island, beyond which lay the Ferguson Passage. Jack thought the men could make one more swim, but it would have to be accomplished in daylight. There was a chance they would be seen by the Japanese. There was also a chance the enemy had lookouts on Olasana Island. The risk was worth the reward, though. Olasana had far more trees to provide cover, and more coconuts. Most important of all, Olasana was much closer to Ferguson Passage.

For the second time, the men slipped into the blue water.

Jack led the way, towing McMahon. Ensign Thom was in charge of the others, once again using the wooden plank from PT 109 to keep them all together. It took several hours to cross to Olasana Island, but they all made it. The men collected their small group on the southernmost tip of the island, hidden in the trees, and conferred among themselves about what should be done next. They agreed it was too risky to explore the rest of the island. If the Japanese had an outpost there, they might walk right into them. The crew chose to remain where they were, hidden amid the trees.

The men gathered and ate more coconuts, though Jack and McMahon both became sick to their stomachs. No one found any fresh water. Frustrated at being so desperately hungry, Ross grabbed a sea snail off the sand and wolfed it down, but the taste was so bitter he immediately made a face. Someone grabbed a land crab, thought better of it (they were mostly just bone and shell), and tossed it back onto the beach. Drained from their ordeal, they all rested. When night came, no one ventured out to sea to signal an American boat. As the men slept, just a few miles away, the PT boats returned to Ferguson Passage searching for Japanese ships.

That night a tropical rain poured down through the darkness. It was a blessing for the thirsty survivors. They awoke from their sleep and opened their mouths to try to catch as much water as possible. McMahon struggled to his feet and moved into the pitch-black jungle to lick the fresh rainwater off the leaves of plants. Unable to use his scorched hands, it was the best he could do to quench his burning thirst.

Suddenly, he stopped cold in his tracks. Just a few yards away he saw a man, outlined in the darkness, looking at him. McMahon was sure he had been seen. The mysterious stranger also froze. McMahon was unarmed and gripped by terror. If the enemy had a patrol on this island, they had been discovered. Yet the man didn't appear to be carrying a weapon. Then he realized it was just Maguire. He was out in the darkness licking the leaves like McMahon, and they had simply stumbled into each other. The two men counted their lucky stars they would live to see the dawn.

In the morning, Jack assembled Thom and Ross on the beach away from the others and asked them, "What should we do now?" The officers debated quietly among themselves what their options were. Jack had made careful decisions since the collision, trying to keep the men alive, leading them to Plum Pudding Island, posting lookouts, and making two attempts to signal for help. Jack knew the enlisted men needed something to give them hope. It was critical the officers do something to improve their situation. Luckily, Jack had an idea.

Half a mile to the south was Naru Island, the last in the small chain of islands before the deep waters of Ferguson Passage. Jack wanted to take Ross and scout the island. American boats would not be out in daylight, but who knew what they might find on Naru. It was possible, and even likely, that the enemy had lookouts watching the channel, yet Jack thought it was worth the risk. Anything was better than sitting and doing nothing while the men suffered. Ross and Thom agreed it was the logical choice.

Jack and Ross easily made the half-mile swim. With great caution, they advanced across the beach. Naru was only four hundred yards long and quite narrow. If the enemy did have lookouts there, Jack and Ross wanted to see them first so they could escape unseen. The two officers moved slowly and as quietly as possible. All they could hear was the rush of the wind and the roar of the waves crashing over the reef on the southern edge of the island.

When they looked out over the ocean toward the south, they could see the mountain on Rendova Island, their home base, thirty-eight miles away. Safety was tantalizingly close, yet still so far away. With no boat or radio, without even a signal flare, Jack and his survivors would remain on their island prison. The officers set out to search the little island for anything useful.

Walking the beach toward the east, they saw a half-sunken Japanese barge out on the reef. It appeared to have been destroyed by Allied aircraft. It rested against the reef in shallow water almost a mile from where they stood. Did the crew of that vessel make it to shore? Were Jack and Ross not alone on the island? It was a gamble, but they continued their search. Jack had his revolver with him. It had only three rounds left—not much if they ran into trouble.

Washed ashore, half buried in the sand, was a rope-bound wooden crate with Japanese writing on it. Jack and Ross tore it open. To their great joy, it was full of Japanese crackers and candy. Delighted, they ate a few, enjoying the taste of their first real food in four days. They carefully saved the rest to take back to the others.

A few steps into the jungle they found an even better prize. Tucked away in the bushes were a dugout canoe and a large metal tin. Carefully opening the tin, Jack's heart jumped. It was fresh water! They both allowed themselves one gulp. This water could keep them all alive for a few more days. And though the canoe could carry only one man, they could use it to move the supplies back to Olasana. What luck! (Although Jack and Ross didn't know it at the time, they had stumbled across a secret supply stash, left behind by the Coastwatchers' scouts.)

As Jack and Ross walked back onto the beach, they froze. Out on the reef, two Islanders were examining the Japanese wreck. The distance was great, but they were sure the two strangers had seen them. Jack and Ross waved to them to come closer. There was a good chance the young men were friendly to the Allies. This could be their chance to escape back to Allied lines and safety! But when the Islanders saw them, they fled to their canoe, paddling away as fast as they could.

Biuku Gasa and Eroni Kumana photographed in 1962 re-creating their approach to Olasana Island.

CHAPTER 15

Fortune sides with him who dares.

—Virgil

Biuku and Eroni were returning to Sepo Island when they saw the Japanese wreck stranded on the reef by Naru Island. The half-sunken barge might hide secrets the Allies could use. They paddled their canoe over and anchored it next to the wreck. Poking through the enemy boat, they searched through all kinds of items, tools, charts, and other gear that was strewn about. They found two rifles that would be useful and each took one before making their way back to the canoe.

As they got into the water, they were startled to see two men back on the beach, watching them. The men were quite

far off, so they couldn't see if they were Japanese or Allies.
Biuku and Eroni were terrified they had been spotted by
the marooned Japanese crew of the vessel they had just
searched. Would the enemy open fire? The scouts fled to
their canoe so quickly that Eroni dropped his newly found
rifle into the surf.

Biuku and Eroni paddled frantically south into Ferguson
Passage. Once they were out of sight, they turned to the
northwest and skirted Leorava Island into Blackett Strait,
heading toward Sepo Island. They still had a long way to go,
and both were tired after paddling so hard to get away from
the strangers on the beach.

Biuku was thirsty from all their hard charging to escape
the men on the beach, and he knew it was still a long way
to Sepo Island. "Let us pull in to shore," he said to Eroni. "I
want to get a drink." Eroni turned the canoe toward the nearest land—Olasana Island. They headed for the southern tip of
Olasana, right where Jack's crew was hiding in the trees.

. . . .

Ensign Thom was in command of the men on Olasana
while Jack and Ross scouted Naru. As they hid in the jungle near the beach, Thom and several others saw a canoe
with two boys approaching right toward them from the sea.
Astounded, they began asking one another in hushed voices,

who could they be? Not all the Islanders were friends of the Allies. It was known that the enemy would pay money to anyone who brought them Allied prisoners.

There was no way to tell if these young men were friend or foe. Thom had several options. They could open fire to prevent the boys from reporting their presence on Olasana to the enemy. He could order his men to stay low and fall back deeper into the jungle to avoid being seen. Or the third option, probably the riskiest one, was to walk toward them and try to communicate. Maybe these two boys could be their salvation. It was Thom's decision to make, and with all their lives at stake, he stood up and walked onto the beach.

Biuku was in the surf, walking the canoe toward shore, when he looked up and saw what must have been a terrible shock to him. A raggedly dressed giant of a man was walking toward them, beckoning them to come closer and calling to them. Biuku shouted a warning to Eroni in the canoe, and they paddled frantically backward away from the beach. The young scouts had never seen anyone as big as this man, nor anyone with blond hair before. Now there was a blond giant of a man standing over six feet tall, shouting to them in English.

More men appeared, yet none of them had weapons. "Come! Come," yelled the big man. The scouts feared for their lives, afraid they had been discovered by the Japanese. The strange men wore uniforms and were well tanned, just like the enemy. Yet they spoke English. Could it be a trick? And how could this giant man have blond hair?

Biuku later remembered, "I said to my friend, 'We are dead men; that is a Japanese.' But the man heard the word *Japan*, and he quickly said, 'I am not a Japanese, but an American.' But I said, 'No, you are Japanese.' But the man called again, 'Look at my skin; it is white; I am not [Japanese.]'" Biuku and Eroni knew if they guessed wrong and the strangers were the enemy, both of them would be killed. So they turned their canoe and began paddling away.

Desperate to stop them, Thom yelled, "Navy! Navy! Americans! Americans!" The scouts turned their canoe to listen, yet they remained afraid and shook their heads. Thom had an idea and pointed to the sky. "White star! White star!" Thom yelled, referring to the markings on all the American aircraft. Now Biuku and Eroni understood. With the few words of English they knew, they remembered that Lieutenant Evans had told them to help anyone from a "white star" aircraft and bring them with all speed back to him. They realized these must be the American sailors they had been told to look for.

Biuku and Eroni paddled back to the shore, where the Americans helped pull their heavy canoe up onto the beach. Then they all shook hands. There is a meaning behind this custom that is often forgotten today. Shaking hands is a sign of peace as well as a greeting. It means, "I meet you, unarmed—I mean you no harm." In the true sense of that purpose, this first meeting between Biuku and Eroni with the marooned survivors of PT 109 was one between friends, even though they could barely understand one another.

When they had moved the canoe under cover, Biuku and Eroni met Zinser and McMahon, who had not gone to the beach. They saw that these men had been badly burned. The scouts then shared what little food they had with the starving Americans, just a handful of yams and a few cigarettes to smoke. Biuku later said of the experience, "Many of them had burns on their bodies and were in great distress. I was very sorry for them . . . So I said to Eroni, 'We must not leave them; if they die, let us die with them.'"

In the few words of English they knew and a lot of gesturing, the scouts explained to the Americans that the enemy was close by—on Naru Island. Biuku and Eroni had just come from there, and claimed to have seen two enemy soldiers. Thom and the others panicked, for they feared Jack and Ross would be captured.

Ensign Thom decided their best chance at being rescued would be to take one of the scouts with him and Starkey in the dugout canoe and immediately make out for the PT boat base at Rendova. If there were Japanese on Naru, it was too risky to swim over and look for Jack and Ross. There were thirty-eight miles of ocean between Olasana and Rendova, but Thom believed they could make it. Biuku and Eroni strongly disagreed. Their canoe would have a hard time carrying anyone the size of Ensign Thom, and the wind and waves had picked up offshore.

Still, Thom overruled the young scouts. Together with Starkey and Biuku, the three paddled outside the reef and headed southeast toward Rendova. Once outside the shelter of the reef, however, the waves threatened to overturn their small boat. Biuku yelled above the wind that they needed to turn back. Thom realized the Islanders had been right all along. It was too dangerous in those sea conditions to try to make a deep-water passage, so they returned to Olasana. They would have to find another way.

•••

Back on Naru, Jack and Ross found nothing else of interest. The two young men they had seen earlier that day had not returned, and there was no sign of Japanese either. Jack wanted to take advantage of having the one-man canoe and paddle into Ferguson Passage that night to try to signal an American boat. Once again, out in the channel, no boats appeared, so Jack returned to Naru to collect the food and water they had discovered and take it back to his men. He found Ross fast asleep on the sand. Jack decided to let him get some rest, and that he would return later to fetch him.

When Jack arrived at the beach on Olasana well after midnight, the men called out to him that two Islanders had found them. He ran to Biuku and Eroni to embrace them warmly. Unlike the others, Jack spoke some of the pidgin the Islanders used to speak with their English governors. He asked if it had been them he had seen off Naru earlier that day. Why had they fled when they had seen Jack and Ross? Biuku explained that they had thought the two Americans were shipwrecked Japanese sailors. Jack felt instinctively that the young men could be trusted.

As for Biuku and Eroni, they liked Jack right away. Not only could he speak with them, but he treated them kindly and with respect. The scouts knew they would do whatever it took to help the Americans, but the language barrier was too great to explain they were scouts for Lieutenant Evans and the Coastwatchers. It was too late to take any action that night, so Biuku and Eroni would remain with the Americans overnight.

The men feasted on the Japanese crackers and candy Jack had discovered, while Thom rationed out small portions of their water supply from the tin. They all settled down for their fourth night marooned behind enemy lines. A few of the crew pretended to sleep while keeping an eye on Biuku and Eroni, whom they didn't quite trust. They were still unsure if the two men would help them escape the island.

• •

On Friday, August 6, Jack woke early to find the men gathered around a small fire the scouts had made by rubbing two sticks together. But the mood of the group was poor. During the night, in a moment of weakness, someone in Jack's crew had drunk all the water that remained in the tin. Once again, they were without any fresh water to drink.

The time had come to plan their next move. Jack now had a canoe and the help of the Islanders. He felt he could trust them with their lives. Taking Biuku and Eroni in their canoe back to Naru, they came across Ross, who was swimming to join the others. Since the small canoe could not hold four people, they towed Ross hanging on to the end of the boat and made for Naru. Once there, the scouts led them to another secret stash, this one hiding a two-man canoe.

Jack took them to the beach facing south across Ferguson Passage, with Rendova Peak on the horizon. The PT boat base at Lumbari was there near Rendova Peak. Jack felt he had no other choice but to send the scouts all the way to Rendova to deliver a message for help. It was their last chance. He knew that in a day or two, McMahon and the others would start dying one by one from their infected wounds, exhaustion, exposure to the sun, thirst, and starvation.

"Come here," Jack said to Biuku. He pointed to the distant mountaintop. "Rendova, Rendova." Biuku understood and nodded. Jack gestured he needed to write a message, but what could he write on? Biuku had an idea. He told Eroni to climb a tree and fetch a coconut. Sharpening a wooden stake at both ends, he planted it deep into the ground and used the point to remove the outer husk from the softer, smooth inner shell of the coconut.

Triumphantly, Biuku handed the smooth coconut back to Jack and pointed at the outer shell. Biuku remembered, "I called to Captain Kennedy and said, 'All right, you write your letter.' And he said, 'Can I write on this?' and I replied, 'Yes, you can.' So he got out his pocketknife and wrote, and then tried to rub it out but could not. He was very surprised that I had invented a new thing to write on!" Jack carved the following message:

NARU ISL

NATIVE KNOWS POSIT

HE CAN PILOT 11 ALIVE NEED SMALL BOAT

KENNEDY

Kennedy's coconut message, which he later had encased in glass and used as a paperweight in the Oval Office.

Back on Olasana, Thom had come to the same conclusion: They must trust the scouts to deliver a message. Maguire discovered a pencil stub in his pocket. Scrounging around their small area, someone found an old Burns Philp steamship company invoice—just what Thom needed! He penciled this message on the scrap of paper:

To Commanding Officer—Oak 0

From: Crew P.T. 109 (Oak 14)

Subject: Rescue of 11 men lost since Sunday, Aug 1st in enemy action. Native knows our position and will bring P.T. boat back to small islands of Ferguson Passage off Naru Island. A small boat is needed to take men off as some are seriously burned.

Signal at night—three dashes.

Password—Roger—Answer—Wilco.

If attempted at day time—advise air coverage or a PBY [a twin-engine flying boat] could set down. Please work out a suitable plan and rely on native boys to any extent.

LJ Thom

Ens. U.S.N.R. Exec 109

When Jack and the others returned from Naru, the officers agreed this was the best course of action. Still, it was a great risk. If the natives were captured and either of the notes was discovered, it would lead the enemy right to them. If for any reason Biuku and Eroni did not carry out the task, the crew of PT 109 would die on Olasana. But Jack and Thom reasoned this was their best option, given the circumstances. Both messages were hidden with Biuku and Eroni. If they were stopped by the Japanese and the coconut had to be thrown away, the other note might survive.

Jack and the rest of the survivors wished Biuku and Eroni well and looked on as the two paddled off. The crew wondered if they would ever see the young Islanders again. Everyone understood this was probably their last chance to make it off the island alive.

For their part, Biuku and Eroni were willing to risk their lives to help rescue the Americans. They considered themselves brothers-in-arms with their newfound friends. Not only were Biuku and Eroni brave, but they were also smart. Before risking the thirty-eight-mile journey to Rendova, however, they would report to their Coastwatchers' network. They made for the island of Wana Wana, seven miles southeast of Naru.

On Wana Wana Island, Biuku and Eroni met with the Melanesian scout Benjamin Kevu, telling him the situation and showing him the coconut message from Kennedy. Benjamin was older than Biuku and Eroni and had worked as a British civil servant before the war. He spoke fluent English and was one of Lieutenant Evans's most trusted senior scouts.

Benjamin Kevu knew that Evans was moving to a new location on the island of Gomu to gain a better view of enemy movements in Ferguson Passage. Benjamin sent another scout to wait for Evans on Gomu and deliver the news. Next he assigned a third man, John Kari, to help Biuku and Eroni paddle to Rendova in a larger canoe. The three scouts would travel through the night to try to reach Rendova as quickly as possible.

That night Lieutenant Evans arrived on schedule to set up his new hideout on Gomu. The messenger told him about the stranded Americans and the mission to reach Rendova by canoe. The heavy and complex radio Evans used would not be set up for hours. He could not signal the Allies for a rescue just yet. Nevertheless, Evans gave orders to his scouts to take immediate action to help the marooned Americans. Soon, night fell and darkness settled over the islands.

Knowing time was running out for his men, Jack returned to Naru in the small canoe to rejoin Ross. Together they would attempt to paddle into Ferguson Passage to try to signal an American boat in the larger two-man canoe Eroni had shown them. The same wind and waves that had forced Thom to abandon his journey to Rendova earlier that day now worried Ross.

He told the skipper, "Gee, I think we'll tip over, Jack, if we go out. It looks a little rough."

But Jack didn't appear concerned. He replied, "Oh, no, it'll be all right . . ."

Using wooden slats from the Japanese crate they had discovered as paddles, the two set out for the reef and the deep water beyond. The wind was howling and the waves crashed over the reef. Ross yelled to Jack that he thought they should give up and go *back* to the beach. Jack responded, shouting, "Barney, I think we ought to go on!"

They made it over the shallow water above the reef and into the channel, where the waves made their small craft uncontrollable. Jack realized Ross had been right: It was too dangerous. "Better turn around and go back!" he yelled above the wind. As they tried to turn the canoe around, a five-foot wave crashed over their side, flipping the canoe over and spilling the two officers into the sea. They quickly grabbed the bottom of the overturned boat as the waves pounded them.

"Sorry I got you out here, Barney!" Jack yelled.

"This would be a great time to say I told you so, but I won't!" Ross yelled back.

The waves pushed them both off the overturned canoe and back into the shallow reef. Jack and Ross became separated in the dark.

"Barney!" Jack yelled into the dark. There was no response. "Barney!"

"I'm over here!" Ross yelled back.

Jack had somehow avoided serious injury, but Ross had cut his right arm and shoulder deeply on the coral. They stood in the shallow water over the reef that led back to the island. Barney was in great pain; his feet were already badly cut from his earlier encounters with the razorlike coral below. Every step was agony.

Luckily, Jack was able to pull the two wooden planks they had used from the surf. Thinking quickly, he laid them down one after the other, on top of the reef's sharp coral, to give Ross something to walk on. Step by step, they slowly made their way back to the beach. It was a miracle they hadn't both drowned. Exhausted from the effort, the sailors collapsed onto the sand and slept. Next to them was the canoe, still intact since it was carved from a single log. Due to the rough seas, no American boats patrolled that night. Their island prison had won yet another round.

John F. Kennedy examines the coconut husk he used to send his secret message.

CHAPTER 16

*What a table was here spread for me in
a wilderness where I saw nothing at first
but to perish for hunger!*

—Daniel Defoe, *Robinson Crusoe*

It was early morning on Saturday, August 7. On Naru Island, Jack and Ross were waking up on the beach after their ordeal the night before. Jack looked out to sea and spied a group of seven Islanders approaching them offshore in a large canoe. Benjamin Kevu was their leader. He came right across the beach to reach them and in flawless English (the King's English at that), Kevu addressed Jack, saying, "I have a letter for you, sir." He handed him a note written on fórmal British stationery. At the top of the page, the letterhead read: ON HIS MAJESTY'S SERVICE. Jack thought this was extremely funny, and he turned to Ross, "You've got to hand it to the British!"

The message was what they had all been praying for:

> To Senior Officer, Naru Island
>
> Friday 11 P.M. Have just learned of your presence on Naru Island and that two natives have taken news to Rendova. I strongly advise you return immediately to here in this canoe and by the time you arrive here I will be in radio communication with authorities at Rendova and we can finalize plans to collect the balance of your party.
>
> A.R. Evans Lt.
>
> RANVR [Royal Australian Naval Volunteer Reserve]

Jack and Ross boarded the canoe with the scouts and crossed to Olasana Island. When the others saw them approaching, they rejoiced. They knew this was the beginning of a rescue, and that Biuku and Eroni had not let them down. Everyone who was able ran to the canoe and offloaded the supplies their new friends had brought. They quickly moved the supplies and the canoe up into the cover of the trees.

The scouts got busy making a feast for everyone. They had brought a small mountain of supplies, including fresh water, a portable stove, cigarettes, and all kinds of foods:

rice, potatoes, yams, boiled fish, C-rations, and beef hash. They even made a lean-to shelter for McMahon to keep him out of the sun. To the men's delight, the Islanders appeared to have little concern for lighting a cooking fire, which meant that they did not think the Japanese were anywhere close by. Perhaps, at last, the PT 109 survivors could truly relax as they enjoyed their first real meal in six days.

· ·

Rather than traveling to the more distant Rendova Island, Biuku and Eroni, with the help of their fellow scout John Kari, had paddled to the nearest American base at Roviana Island off the coast of New Georgia. The U.S. Army had an artillery base there to support the Allies fighting to capture Munda. As the Melanesian rescue party helped the Americans on Olasana Island, these three scouts—Biuku Gasa, Eroni Kumana, and John Kari—showed an American officer Jack's message on the coconut and the note penciled by Ensign Thom. The officer didn't know Jack or Thom, but he knew the navy had a PT boat base at Rendova across the channel. He radioed the navy and asked them to send over a PT boat to pick up the scouts.

By the time the scouts were delivered to Rendova, the base was alive with excitement over a radio message that had been relayed to them from Lieutenant Evans back on

Gomu sent at 9:30 a.m.

> ELEVEN SURVIVORS PT BOAT ON NARU ISLAND—
> HAVE SENT FOOD AND LETTER ADVISING SENIOR
> OFFICER TO COME HERE WITHOUT DELAY—WARN
> AVIATION OF CANOES CROSSING FERGUSON

As if by magic, the three Islanders appeared with their own messages from Jack and Thom. Biuku and Eroni had fulfilled their promise to Jack. They had paddled through more than thirty miles of enemy-held water to deliver his message. Now the U.S. Navy would leap into action to rescue the men they thought had been lost. At 11:30 a.m., the base commander at Rendova had a reply radioed to Lieutenant Evans.

> GREAT NEWS—COMMANDER PT BASE RECEIVED A
> MESSAGE JUST AFTER YOURS FROM SURVIVORS BY
> NATIVES—THEY GAVE THEIR POSITION AND NEWS
> THAT SOME ARE BADLY WOUNDED AND REQUEST
> RESCUE—THEY WOULD SEND SURFACE CRAFT TO
> MEET YOUR RETURNING CANOES OR ANYTHING
> YOU ADVISE—THEY WISH TO EXPRESS GREAT
> APPRECIATION—WE WILL AWAIT YOUR ADVICE

After everyone had eaten a wonderful meal, it was time for Jack to make his way to Gomu Island to meet Lieutenant Evans and plan a rescue. Jack didn't like the idea of leaving his men, but the Islanders could take only one American back with them. Jack was the most experienced sailor among the crew. He knew he could guide a PT boat through the reef to Olasana Island, even in the dark. He was determined to do just that, so Jack agreed to go with the seven scouts to Gomu, hidden in their canoe.

Once in Blackett Strait, Jack lay down in the canoe. The Islanders hid him under some burlap sacks and palm tree fronds. When they were far out into the channel, they all heard aircraft approaching.

"What's going on?" Jack asked Benjamin from under his hiding place.

"Japanese planes," Benjamin replied. "Stay down!"

Three enemy fighters were overhead circling their canoe, scanning for anything suspicious. If they saw Jack hidden under the palm leaves, the enemy would swoop down and kill them all. Benjamin took a gamble and stood up, waving at one of the enemy planes. The trick worked, and the enemy fighters departed for Kolombangara. Elated by their success, the Islanders all broke into song as they paddled.

By 6:00 p.m., the seven loyal scouts had made their way to Gomu. Jack waited until they were at the beach to come out from his hiding place to meet Lieutenant Evans. By this time, Jack had been marooned for six days. He was bearded and sunburned, half starved and wearing tattered shorts, with his legs and feet covered in cuts and bruises.

"Hello, I'm Kennedy," Jack said as the two men shook hands.

Evans motioned toward his camp. "Come and have some tea."

Earlier that afternoon, Evans had received a radio message from the PT boat base at Rendova.

THREE PT BOATS PROCEED TONIGHT AND WILL BE AT NARU ISLAND ABOUT TEN PM—THEY WILL TAKE RAFTS ETC—WILL INFORM YOU WHEN WE RECEIVE ADVICE OF RESCUE

Evans didn't want Kennedy to risk going back to the island. He thought that the PT boats should go in and pick up the survivors of PT 109 without him. Jack disagreed. It would be difficult to spot his men in the dark unless the PT boat skipper knew exactly where they were. It would also be hard to navigate the surrounding reefs without a guide. Jack could perform those tasks. More than that, Jack was their commanding officer. It was his duty to remain with his men until they were delivered to safety. He told Evans they could meet the PT boats on their way to Naru and he would guide them in.

Lieutenant Evans radioed the plan to the Navy base at Rendova.

LIEUTENANT KENNEDY CONSIDERS IT ADVISABLE THAT HE PILOT PT BOATS TONIGHT—HE WILL AWAIT BOATS NEAR PATPARAN ISLAND—PT BOAT TO APPROACH ISLAND FROM NW TEN PM AS CLOSE AS POSSIBLE—BOAT TO FIRE FOUR SHOTS AS RECOGNITION—HE WILL ACKNOWLEDGE WITH SAME AND GO ALONGSIDE IN CANOE—SURVIVORS NOW ON ISLAND NW OF NARU

As Jack was preparing to leave that evening to meet the American PT boats, he realized his revolver had only three shots left. Ross had fired three of his six shots, trying to signal for help in Ferguson Passage several nights earlier. Evans gave him a captured Japanese rifle and some coveralls to wear. It was time to head out.

A little after 10:00 p.m., Jack sat with several scouts in a canoe near Patparan Island. They heard the deep rumble of powerful engines approaching. Four shots rang out from the dark. Jack stood and fired the last three rounds from his revolver into the air. Then he picked up the Japanese rifle and fired a single, fourth shot into the air. The kick from the powerful rifle almost knocked Jack out of the canoe. In moments, their canoe was alongside the eighty-foot side of PT 157, which was commanded by Jack's friend Lieutenant William Liebenow and escorted by PT 171, which was skippered by Lieutenant Arthur Berndtson.

"Hey, Jack!" called Liebenow.

The stress from a week of life-or-death survival came over Jack and he yelled up to Liebenow, "Where the hell

Lieutenant William Liebenow.

have you been?" Jack was angry that no one had come back for them on the night of August 2. He believed that you should never leave men behind.

Benjamin Kevu reached down and helped Jack board the PT boat from the canoe. Jack was greeted by his commanding officer from Motor Torpedo Boat Squadron 2, Lieutenant Al Cluster, and a fellow skipper and close friend, Lieutenant Henry Brantingham, from PT 159. Alongside the officers were the beaming Biuku and Eroni, and several newspaper reporters who got wind of a great story and managed to hitch a ride.

Two hours later, Jack had guided them through the dangerous reefs around Olasana Island to within yelling distance of the beach.

"Lenny! Hey, Lenny!" Jack yelled from PT 157. It was nearly pitch-black out. The survivors on the island had been sleeping. Then voices were heard, and the PT boat shut down its engines. A rubber dinghy (a small inflatable rubber boat) was sent to the beach to find the men. Soon it was back carrying two of Jack's crew. The survivors were brought out two at a time and carefully pulled onto the deck of the boat. They were not out of danger yet—if the enemy discovered them, PT 157 was a sitting duck. Immediately after the last man had boarded, the engines roared back to life, and they were off again, this time for the safety of home.

The medics seeing to the men's needs obeyed a naval regulation that anyone rescued from being shipwrecked was to be issued several rations of brandy. As PT 157 sped toward the safety of the base at Rendova, one of the PT 109 crew, William Johnston, discovered that Biuku and Eroni had studied under missionary teachers. With the rum flowing through their veins, Biuku and Eroni, along with the men from PT 109, broke into song:

> *Jesus loves me! This I know,*
> *For the Bible tells me so;*
> *Little ones to him belong,*
> *They are weak but he is strong.*
> *Yes, Jesus loves me!*

Meanwhile, Jack went below deck, unable to rejoice at their good fortune. The six-day ordeal had taken its toll on him. His body was a mass of serious cuts and bruises, his back was injured, and he had a lost a lot of weight. Jack fell into a bunk and wept. He was angry that his fellow PT boat skippers had not returned to find them on the night of August 2. His boat had been lost and two of his crewmen

We rescued Captain Kennedy and his crew from their enemies. This then is my act of love or helpfulness to the big Kingdom, the whole of the U.S.A.

—Biuku Gasa

were dead. What did he have to show for his accomplishments as a PT boat skipper?

When they arrived safely back at the navy base at Rendova, there was a celebration. Eroni remembered years later, "Kennedy and the boys invited us for a small party and thanked us for what we did to them. Kennedy told us, 'If I am alive at the end of the war I promise to visit the two of you or invite the two of you to America.' Then he gave us something like a medal, a piece of decoration from his uniform, one for me and one for Biuku. That is the last time I saw him."

What Kennedy had given to Biuku was his lucky gold coin. It had served him well.

Some of the Islanders who helped rescue Kennedy and his crew (photographed in 1962).

An exhausted and ill Lieutenant Kennedy, photographed just after his return to the United States, December 1944.

PART FOUR

THE ROAD HOME

It's a thing to see when a boy comes home.

—John Steinbeck,
The Grapes of Wrath

Jack Kennedy recovering on Tulagi after the PT 109 rescue, August 1943.

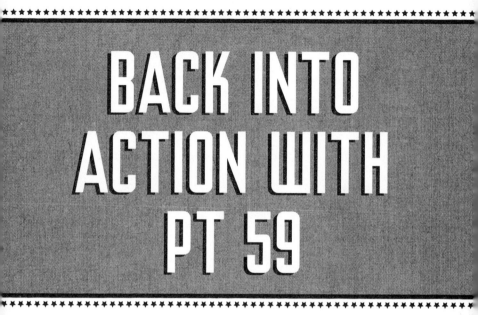

BACK INTO ACTION WITH PT 59

[Jack] proved himself to be very intelligent in the way he ran his boat, as well as cool and courageous under fire.

—Navy Lieutenant Commander Byron White

Jack and his ten surviving crewmen from PT 109 were moved to the island of Tulagi to recover from their ordeal at a navy hospital. McMahon and Johnston were evacuated to Guadalcanal to treat their more serious injuries. Jack took the opportunity to write his parents a quick letter even though it would not reach them for weeks.

Dear Folks,

This is just a short note to tell you that I am alive—and not kicking—in spite of any reports that you may happen to hear. It was believed otherwise for a few days—so reports or rumors may have gotten back to you. Fortunately, they misjudged the durability of a Kennedy—am back at the base now—and am OK. As soon as possible I shall try to give you the whole story. Much love to you all. —Jack

On August 18, the navy approved the news stories written by the reporters who were on PT 159. The story of PT 109 and Jack's heroism was about to make national headlines. This all came as a great surprise to someone very close to Jack—his mother, Rose. At 8:20 the next morning, she was sitting by the radio at home in Hyannis Port when the phone rang. It was someone from the *Boston Globe* newspaper asking if she had anything to comment on Jack being rescued. "Rescued from what?" she asked the caller.

Jack's father, Joseph, had gone horseback riding early that morning and was driving his car back from the stables

Rose Kennedy, Jack's mother, photographed in 1939.

when the story of Jack's rescue came over the radio. He was so surprised he pulled the car off the road and into a field. When he returned home, he told Rose what he had been hiding from her for several weeks. The navy had told him that Jack and the crew of PT 109 were reported missing on August 6. He hadn't had the heart to tell Rose until they were sure what had happened. Luckily, the navy had never sent the next of kin telegrams after all.

On August 20, the *New York Times* headlined, KENNEDY'S SON SAVES 10 IN PACIFIC AS DESTROYER SPLITS HIS PT BOAT. The *Boston Globe* proclaimed, KENNEDY'S SON A HERO IN THE PACIFIC. Jack's heroic deeds (as told to the newsmen by the PT 109 survivors) were briefly a matter of national attention. The story recounted that "Mrs. Kennedy, first to hear the news by telephone at their summer home, expressed deep sorrow for the two crewmen who lost their lives." Phone calls, telegrams, and letters of congratulations flooded the Kennedy home.

At the field hospital on Tulagi, Jack did not feel like a hero—he felt like a failure. He had not managed to strike a single blow against the enemy, and his PT 109 had been lost with two of his crew. But instead of wallowing in sorrow for himself, he remembered the lesson his father had drilled into him and all his brothers and sisters from childhood: "There are no whiners in this house!" Jack's commanding officer from Motor Torpedo Boat Squadron 2 told him that it was a navy custom that if a sailor lost his ship in battle he would be allowed to return to shore duty in America. Jack could return to the United States for a comfortable and safe job for the rest of the war—a golden ticket home.

But Jack refused to leave Tulagi. He wanted to return to sea and continue the fight against the Japanese. At that time, the Navy was converting a few PT boats by removing their torpedoes and rearming them with heavier cannon and machine guns. They would serve as gunboats to take the fight close to enemy shores. The Japanese navy had given up supplying their islands via the Tokyo Express and were now using heavy barges. On September 1, three weeks after the PT 109 rescue, Jack was given command of PT 59, the first of the new gunboats.

Joseph Kennedy hoped Jack would return home after such a close call on PT 109, and because of Jack's history with a bad back. Knowing his father would not approve, Jack covered up the fact that he had been offered a chance to go home, writing in a letter, "They will not send anyone back while there is fighting in this area—when it's over—I'll get back . . . As a matter of fact—I am in a bad spot for getting out as am now Captain of a gunboat . . . so I will have to stick around and try to make a go of it." No matter what, Jack was not a quitter.

Jack's new command was a seventy-seven-foot Elco, older than PT 109 but completely overhauled. The torpedo tubes, depth charges, and 20mm cannon were replaced by twin 40mm cannon fore and aft, plus five .50-caliber machine guns on both the starboard and port sides. Armor plating was also installed to protect the crew, and unlike PT 109, Jack's new boat had radar. They would be hunting for Japanese barges, up to sixty feet long, carrying as many as a hundred soldiers or tons of supplies. Since the barges were of shallow draft (their hulls did not sit deeply in the water), torpedoes were useless against them. The enemy armed their barges with machine guns and cannon of their own.

To locate the barges, PT boats had to move close to enemy-held islands at night and risk grounding on the hundreds of uncharted reefs within range of enemy guns on land. Traveling in groups, the barges were heavily armed. Hunting them was a dangerous mission for the new PT gunboats, yet it was the only way to stop enemy movement among the islands. By then the Japanese knew the mission of American PT boats was to attack their supply craft and nicknamed their dangerous foes "Devil Boats."

On October 8, Jack was promoted to full lieutenant. PT 59 was ready for action, but Jack still needed a crew. To his great surprise, some old friends showed up. Edgar Mauer and John Maguire, who had both survived the PT 109 collision with Jack, arrived at the dock to see him.

"What are you doing here?" asked Kennedy.

"What kind of guy are you?" they replied. "You got a boat and didn't come get us?"

Maguire later said, "It was the nearest I ever seen him come to crying." The three PT 109 crewmen who had served on PT 109 before the collision also volunteered: Maurice Kowal, Edmund Drewitch, and Leon Drawdy. Jack's new executive officer was veteran Lieutenant Robert Lee Rhoads. PT 59 had so many additional guns the crew had jumped from twelve to sixteen officers and enlisted men. The time had come to get back into the action.

The war had not stood still while Jack and his PT 109 crew were marooned behind enemy lines, or during the six weeks they spent readying PT 59 for action. The key Japanese position at Munda had fallen to the Allies on August 6, with the islands of Gizo and Vella Lavella following a week later, on August 15. But the Japanese still held on to the last two major islands in the Solomons: Bougainville and Choiseul. If the Allies captured Bougainville, their aircraft would be within striking range of Japan's main fortress in the southwest Pacific at Rabaul, on the island of New Britain, one hundred and fifty miles to the northwest.

A PT boat base was quickly established at the village of Lambu Lambu on the island of Vella Lavella. On October 18, PT 59 left Tulagi and sailed past the same islands of the PT 109 adventure: Plum Pudding, Olasana, Naru,

Kolombangara, and Gizo, making its way to Lambu Lambu Cove, the men's new base of operations. The plan was for other PT boats to escort one gunboat as they hunted Japanese barges close to shore at night. The enemy had suffered many defeats, but they had no intention of giving up.

For the next month, Jack led PT 59 on thirteen patrols off the island of Choiseul and was attacked by Japanese aircraft several times. Japanese barges were like phantoms, hugging the island shore on the blackest nights and almost impossible to see in total darkness. On just one patrol, PT 59 encountered three enemy barges that quickly disappeared into an invisible cove as soon as the American boats opened fire. The PT boats did not dare to get any closer or follow them.

Finally, on November 2, 1943, the chance came that Jack had been waiting for all his life—to make a difference. The Allies had just landed a major force on the island of Bougainville, about eighty miles northwest of Vella Lavella. To trick the Japanese into believing the target of the invasion was elsewhere, six hundred marines were landed on the island of Choiseul twenty miles to the southeast of Bougainville a few days earlier. Those brave marines faced over three thousand Japanese troops.

Word came that a patrol of over fifty marines had been nearly surrounded with their backs to the sea. Two Allied

landing craft were sent to withdraw the men off the beach, and two PT boats were requested to help. There was one major problem since PT 59 was in the middle of refueling and her tanks were only one-third full. It would take hours to finish refueling and there was no time. Jack had just enough fuel to get them to the marines' location and part of the way back to base. If they went on this dangerous mission, PT 236 would have to tow PT 59 home.

But still Jack didn't hesitate. He would go into the breach once again to help others.

....

The marine patrol on Choiseul was in a desperate situation. They had encountered a much larger Japanese force and had to retreat down the Warrior River to the sea. With thirty minutes of daylight remaining, they saw the two landing craft that had been sent to rescue them. The boats were a hundred yards off the beach, unable to get closer because of the sharp coral reef. The enemy was closing in, intent on finishing off the trapped marines. As if by magic, a rain squall began that hid the Americans from enemy fire as they waded out to the boats—their only chance to escape.

As the marines piled into the landing craft, it sank deeper into the shallow water. When they tried to pull back off the reef, one of the boats ripped open its hull against the coral and began flooding, while the other damaged one of its propellers. The marines in the sinking landing craft began to bail with their helmets, but it was no use. They began readying their weapons to wade back toward the beach and fight it out with the enemy. Then they heard the deep rumble of engines in the sea behind them, and through the haze and growing darkness a boat appeared.

"It's a PT boat!" someone shouted, crazy with joy. Jack maneuvered PT 59 up alongside the sinking landing craft, placing his boat between the enemy fire and the stranded marines. Jack's gunners could have opened up with all their guns toward the enemy on the beach, but Jack wasn't sure if any Americans were still in the way. He ordered his gunners to hold their fire. Men from both landing craft scrambled aboard, including a severely wounded marine, Corporal Edward James "Jimmy" Schnell from Wilmette, Illinois.

"Where can we lay this man down?" asked a medic.

"Take him down below," replied Jack.

With all thirty-six marines and three navy crewmen from the wrecked landing craft safe on board PT 59, Jack maneuvered out to sea, escorting the remaining landing craft back to the village of Voza, where the marines had first landed on Choiseul. The marines crammed the deck as PT 59 made its way through the falling darkness. The crew brought out canned peaches, which the marines tore into like hungry wolves. Below deck, laid out on Jack's bunk, the medic worked to try to save the life of young Jimmy Schnell.

When they dropped the marines off at Voza, PT 59 turned and raced for their base on Vella Lavella. The hospital there was the only chance to save Jimmy. Jack looked at their fuel gauge—it read empty. Down below, the medic had opened a fifth bottle of blood plasma to try to help his patient live just a little longer. He was slowly bleeding to death from a bullet through his chest.

"Am I going to be okay?" Jimmy asked the medic. "Do you really think I'll be all right?"

"Sure, I'm working on you, aren't I?" replied the medic. "You've got it made, boy; you're headed for San Diego."

Halfway across the channel to Vella Lavella, PT 59 ran out of fuel. PT 236 threw them a line and began the slow tow back to base. It was risky business being under tow. If an enemy aircraft found them, both boats would be sitting ducks. Luckily, no enemy planes came along that night, and the two boats crept their way back to safety. In the cabin, Jimmy passed away quietly. There was nothing they could do to save him. He was one of nine marines killed on the raid.

Jack had much to be proud of: His mission to rescue the marines had still been a success, despite their losses. They had saved over thirty-nine men from certain death. Neither

None of the hero stuff about me. The real heroes are not the men who return, but those who stay out there, like plenty of them do, two of my men included.
—John F. Kennedy

Jack nor his crew would ever receive a medal or even a mention of valor in the reports for their actions. But Jack had the satisfaction of knowing they had done it right—he had made a difference. It was a measure of confidence he would take with him for the rest of his life.

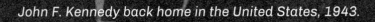
John F. Kennedy back home in the United States, 1943.

THE COSTS OF WAR

*He who wishes to fight must
first count the cost.*

—Sun Tzu, *The Art of War*

Jack's time in the Pacific came to an end in mid-November 1943, when he was relieved of command of PT 59 by his commanding officer and sent to a hospital on Tulagi. He was in terrible shape. Seven months of combat duty in the Solomons and the PT 109 ordeal had taken a severe toll on his health. His back was in constant pain and his stomach felt like it was on fire. He also had come down with malaria and had lost an alarming amount of weight. It was time to go home.

On November 18, 1943, Jack bid farewell to his loyal crew, shaking hands with every man and telling them, "If there is ever anything I can do for you, ask me. You will always know where you can get in touch with me." On December 23, he boarded the escort carrier USS *Breton* for the journey back to San Francisco. Within weeks he was back at his father's estate in Palm Beach, Florida, resting by the pool. A few weeks later, the navy ordered him back to Melville and later Miami as a PT boat instructor.

Jack slid easily back into the life of the rich and famous, but inside he was a far cry from the youthful college boy who had reported for duty in Tulagi only one year earlier. He had proven himself in action to his crew, his family, and most important, to himself. His future was wide open for anything he wanted to do after the war ended. He was considering becoming a college professor since his older brother, Joe Jr., was the one chosen by their father to enter politics after the war.

In February 1944, Jack took a date to a famous nightclub in Manhattan called the Stork Club. There he met up with an old friend, John Hersey, who was a journalist looking for new stories to write. Over drinks, Jack told him about the Solomons and PT 109. John was fascinated. He wanted to publish the story. The next day Jack talked to his father, who thought it was a wonderful idea. If Jack ever wanted to enter public service, a well-known story about him could only help him to be noticed by voters.

John F. Kennedy and friends in Hyannis Port, MA, in 1944. Front, left to right: Edward "Ted" Kennedy and his cousin Joe Gargan. Standing, left to right: Paul "Red" Fay, John F. Kennedy, Leonard J. Thom, Jim Reed, Barney Ross, and Bernie Lyons.

By the end of the month, John Hersey met up with Jack again to interview him for the story. Before he began, Jack suggested Hersey should talk to several of his former crewmen, who were already back at the nearby Melville base. Hersey later wrote of those meetings, "They were wildly

Lieutenant John F. Kennedy receives the Navy and Marine Corps Medal at the Chelsea Naval Hospital, Massachusetts, June 12, 1944.

devoted to him, all of them. Absolutely clear devotion to him by the crew . . . They really did like him."

Hersey's story, "Survival," was first published in *The New Yorker* magazine in June 1944, just after the Allies landed in Normandy on D-Day. Later it would be serialized (reprinted in short chapters over several issues) in *Reader's Digest*, which was read by millions. Joseph Kennedy had succeeded in making the family name famous across the country, and the PT 109 story had taken center stage. It was Hersey's story that made Jack Kennedy a hero in the eyes of the American people.

The navy agreed, and on June 12, 1944, Jack was awarded the Navy and Marine Corps Medal—a decoration honoring life-saving actions in or out of combat. Leonard Thom and Barney Ross received the same medal as well. Jack was also awarded the Purple Heart for the wounds he had suffered during the PT 109 ordeal. Jack never considered himself a hero, but the medals were an important symbol of his courage for other people. He is the only American president to ever receive a Purple Heart.

Sunday, August 13 was hot and muggy at Hyannis Port. The Kennedy family was outside on the sunroom porch after lunch. Most of the young Kennedys were there, including

> I firmly believe, that as much as I was shaped
> by anything, so I was shaped by the hand of fate
> moving in World War II. Of course, the same can
> be said of almost any American or British or
> Australian man of my generation. The war made us.
> It was and is our single greatest moment.
>
> —John F. Kennedy

Jack, who was on leave from the navy. Their father was upstairs taking his afternoon nap.

"Our little family group included Mother, Jack, Joey Gargan and me, and Jean and Eunice . . . ," remembered Ted Kennedy. "We were listening to a recording of Bing Crosby singing the number one tune of that year, 'I'll Be Seeing You,' when a strange dark car pulled into the front driving circle and stopped. Two naval chaplains got out, walked up the steps to the porch, and knocked on the screen door. Mother looked up from the Sunday paper she'd been reading in a tiny rocking chair that only she could fit into. As she received the clerics, we could hear a few words: 'missing— lost.' All of us froze."

They asked to speak to Mr. Kennedy. Moments later, Joseph and Rose came back onto the porch. Ted remembered, "Dad's face was twisted. He got the words out that confirmed what we already suspected. Joe Jr. was dead."

"Your brother Joe has been lost," their father announced, choking back tears. "He died flying a volunteer mission. I want you all to be particularly good to your mother." Then he went upstairs so his children would not see him cry. It was a shock from which he would never truly recover, and it would not be the last tragedy his family would face.

Joe Jr. had volunteered to fly a top-secret mission to try to destroy a heavily defended German fortification on the coast of France. The Germans were launching V-1 and

Ensign Joseph P. Kennedy Jr. at the Squantum Naval Air Station in Massachusetts, where he started training on July 15, 1941.

Jack and Ted Kennedy at Hyannis Port in 1946.

V–2 "Vengeance" rockets into London since the Allies had invaded Normandy on June 6. Joe Jr. had already finished his tour of duty in Europe and was scheduled to return home, but the navy offered him the mission to try to stop the German rockets from killing thousands of British people. He told a friend in his last phone call, "If I don't come back, tell my dad that I love him very much."

Everyone sobbed in grief for a long time. Then Jack spoke up. "Joe wouldn't want us sitting here crying. He would want us to go sailing. Let's go sailing. Teddy, Joey, get the sails. We're going sailing." When they returned, Jack ended up walking alone for a long time on the beach in front of his father's house. The weight of grief over the sudden loss of his beloved older brother must have been crushing, but so too was the realization that he was now the oldest Kennedy son.

John F. Kennedy photographed at his 11th district headquarters in Boston, 1946.

ROAD TO THE WHITE HOUSE

When he came into the room he was like the sun: He radiated confidence and victory.

—Pedro Sanjuan, U.S. State Department,
speaking about John F. Kennedy

Jack was medically discharged from the navy in March 1945 because of the injuries to his back. He went to work as a newspaper writer for his father's friend William Randolph Hearst. Germany surrendered to the Allies on May 7, and Japan announced its surrender on August 15, following the atomic bombings of Hiroshima and Nagasaki. Jack was in Europe covering events for the newspapers, but soon became bored with just writing about events. He wanted to have a voice in what was happening on the world's stage.

His first chance to be elected to public office came in the fall of 1946, when he ran for Congress in Boston's 11th district. This was a challenge for Jack. He was just twenty-nine years old, had never served in government before, and had not even lived in the working-class district whose interests he hoped to represent in Congress. Besides a famous name

Jack Kennedy casting his vote in the primary election for the 11th district in Boston, MA. He was accompanied by his grandparents Mr. and Mrs. John F. Fitzgerald. (June 18, 1946)

(his father had been an ambassador to Great Britain and his grandfather John Francis Fitzgerald had been mayor of Boston and served in the U.S. House of Representatives), how could he connect with voters? The answer—Jack's wartime record and the PT 109 story.

Jack was presented to the public as a decorated war hero, returning home to a new challenge to serve his home state of Massachusetts. War veterans who had also just returned home identified with him. Gold Star mothers who had lost their sons or daughters in the war sympathized with him and his family. Younger voters admired Jack's courage and that he represented something new in government. When the votes were cast in November, Jack won his first political seat in the House of Representatives.

When Jack Kennedy entered his next

★ WORLD WAR II ★
Facts and Trivia

GOLD STAR MOTHERS

During World War II, American families with loved ones serving in the armed forces would hang a service pendant in their window with a blue star for each family member in uniform. If someone was killed, the blue star would be replaced by a gold one. "Gold Star mothers" were those who had lost a son or a daughter in the service of the United States.

political race to win a Senate seat in the fall of 1952, the stakes were much higher. Now he would have to win votes across his entire state, not just from the Boston area, where he was a local hero. Once again, the PT 109 story became the central part of his campaign. Thousands of copies of the Hersey PT 109 story were distributed in pamphlet form to the public.

A year earlier, Jack had visited Tokyo at the end of an Asian diplomatic tour. He asked his Japanese host, Professor Gunji Hosono, if he could help him find the captain who commanded the destroyer that collided with PT 109. Jack had no idea who he was, where he lived, or even the name of the ship they had encountered in the Solomons. But Jack wanted to find him. It would be a powerful political symbol of reconciliation between countries, for enemies to become friends. It would mean a lot to Jack personally as well.

In October 1952, at the height of his race for the Senate, Jack received a remarkable letter, delivered by a mutual friend of Professor Hosono. Kohei Hanami, the former captain of the Japanese destroyer *Amagiri*, had written a friendly letter of introduction and praised Jack's courage under fire during the PT 109 sinking. He also endorsed Jack as a candidate for the U.S. Senate. The letter was made public to help Jack win the election a month later, in a narrow victory against Republican senator Henry Cabot Lodge Jr.

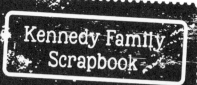

From a letter by Captain Kohei Hanami to John F. Kennedy, September 15, 1952

Dear Mr. Kennedy,

I am informed by Dr. Gunji Hosono that a warship sunk by a destroyer of the Japanese navy during the Solomon Islands Battle in August 1943 was under your command. This is a big surprise to me as I happened to be the Commander of the destroyer which sunk your ship . . .

In one of the night battle in early August 1943, I sighted a bold enemy boat of small size was heading directly toward my destroyer of a larger type. Having

no time to exchange gunfire as the ships came so close to each other, my destroyer had to directly hit the enemy boat, slicing in two. To my great surprise this boat happened to be the P.T. boat which was under your command.

I take this opportunity to pay my profound respect to your daring and courageous action in this battle and also to congratulate you upon your miraculous escape under such circumstances.

I regret very much that I missed the opportunity of meeting you during your last visit to Japan . . . I am looking forward to seeing you in your next visit to Japan.

I . . . know from Time magazine that you are going to run for the next election of Senators. I am firmly convinced that a person who practices tolerance to the former enemy like you, if elected to the high office in your country, would no doubt contribute not only to the promotion of genuine friendship between Japan and the United States but also to the establishment of a universal peace.

I do wish the best of your success in the coming election in your country.

With personal regards,

Kohei Hanami
Former commander of the Destroyer "AMAGIRI"

A year after he was elected to the U.S. Senate, Jack married Jacqueline Lee "Jackie" Bouvier on September 12, 1953. Together they made one of the most dazzling young couples in Washington. They would have two children together,

Jacqueline Bouvier Kennedy and John F. Kennedy cut their wedding cake during their reception at Hammersmith Farm, in Newport, Rhode Island, September 12, 1953.

Caroline and John Jr. With seven years of experience in the Senate, Jack decided the time was right to run for the presidency in 1960. He would be running against the highly intelligent and experienced Richard M. Nixon, who was then serving as the vice president of the United States for president Dwight D. Eisenhower.

Former PT 109 crewman Edmund T. Drewitch met Kennedy on the campaign trail in Champaign, IL, on October 24, 1960.

Once again, the PT 109 saga would play an important role in Jack's chances for election. There had never been a Catholic elected as president, and parts of the country were opposed to a candidate who might be more loyal to the pope in Rome than to the duties of public office. The PT 109 story helped to overcome those fears as proof that Jack was an American loyal first to his country. The story also demonstrated his courage and leadership under fire, which was important to Americans who feared the rising threat of Soviet Communism.

Jack's victory over Richard Nixon in the November 1960 presidential election was the closest ever won. At noon on January 20, 1961, John F. Kennedy was sworn in as the nation's thirty-fifth president. At age forty-three, he was the youngest man in American history to be elected president. In one of the most famous inaugural speeches ever made, Kennedy asked Americans to remain patriotic: "My fellow Americans, ask not what your country can do for you; ask what you can do for your country." He wished to rally the forces of good to battle against the enemies of all mankind: tyranny, poverty, disease, and war itself.

A vast parade down Pennsylvania Avenue followed the inauguration. Among the marching bands and Boy Scouts was a great surprise for Jack—PT 617, an Elco boat repainted with the big white letters *PT 109* on the bow. On deck were his friends, eight of the surviving members of his crew: John Maguire, George Ross, Charles Harris, Ray Starkey, William Johnston, Gerard Zinser, Edgar Mauer, and Maurice Kowal. Jack stood as they passed by, and waved to them the hand signal they had used to start up the engines during the war.

A few days later Jack was visited in the White House by Gunji Hosono and his daughter Haruko. They presented the new president with a message of congratulations from the Japanese prime minister, and a small ceremonial scroll with

John F. Kennedy meeting young Jack Kirksey and his mother in 1960. Jack was the son of Andrew J. Kirksey, who was killed during the PT 109 collision.

Japanese kanji writing. It was a wish for success, signed by veterans of the Japanese destroyer *Amagiri*. On Jack's desk, encased in glass, was his famous coconut message, now an effective presidential paperweight.

Within days, Jack received another letter from Biuku Gasa, transcribed by a Methodist preacher in the Solomons. Biuku expressed his joy that Jack was elected president. He credited their luck at finding Jack and his crew in the islands as an act of Christian faith. "It was not in my strength that

Some of the former PT 109 crewmen who gathered before Kennedy's inaugural parade on January 19, 1961.

I and my friends were able to rescue you in the time of war, but in the strength of God . . ." Jack wrote back saying, "You will always have a special place in my mind and my heart, and I wish you and your people continued prosperity and good health."

Benjamin Kevu (center) and Barney Ross (left) visit with President Kennedy in the Oval Office on September 25, 1962.

Jack always hoped he would see Biuku and Eroni again one day. He also put into motion a plan to visit Japan in 1964, his reelection year, and meet Kohei Hanami and the veterans of the *Amagiri*. Robert Kennedy, Jack's younger brother, traveled to Japan in 1962 to pave the way for the first-ever American presidential visit to that country. During his stay in Japan, Robert met with Hanami and they exchanged gifts. Robert gave Hanami his personal golden tie pin cast in the shape of PT 109, and embossed with the letters KENNEDY 1960.

Robert's goodwill visit to Japan was a huge success. The path was now open for Jack to visit Japan in 1964 and meet Hanami. Jack would have been the first American president in office to visit Japan, but he never got the chance to make that trip. On November 22, 1963, Jack and his wife, Jacqueline, flew to Dallas, Texas, where they drove in an open car in a parade through the city. Thousands upon thousands of people lined the street to see the president and the First Lady, cheering as they drove by.

Waiting in ambush on the sixth floor of a building on Dealey Plaza was an assassin, Lee Harvey Oswald. As Kennedy's car passed below his window, Oswald, a former marine sharpshooter, fired three times, hitting the president twice and killing him instantly. The world watched in disbelief and horror—a moment in time that few Americans who lived through it will ever forget. John F. Kennedy's life had ended, but his legacy lives on.

Jack Kennedy is remembered as one of America's greatest presidents, even though he did not live to serve a second term. People recall his intelligence, his dashing good looks, quick wit, and the ability to move millions of people with his

President Kennedy and the First Lady driving through Dallas moments before he was shot on November 22, 1963.

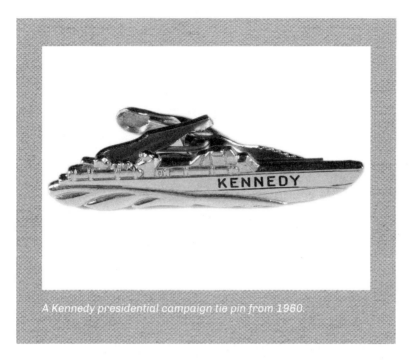

A Kennedy presidential campaign tie pin from 1960.

epic speeches. Above all, people remember Kennedy for his courage, whether it be his stand against Soviet aggression in the Cuban Missile Crisis, founding the Civil Rights Act to protect all Americans from discrimination, creating the Peace Corps, or putting men on the moon with the Apollo space program—all of these challenges took tremendous courage and determination.

Jack's inner strength was forged in those hours and days in the Solomons, trapped behind enemy lines, trying to save his crew from capture and certain death. Jack said the experience shaped him like no other and remained one

President Kennedy photographed with a model of PT 109 at the White House in 1961.

of the greatest defining moments of his life. The war was a crucible—a personal test in which he entered a boy and emerged as a man with the courage and ability to lead others. Jack's wartime experience shaped the character and courage of the man who became the thirty-fifth president of the United States.

Maxwell Kennedy, JFK's nephew, meets Eroni Kumana in 2002.

EPILOGUE

The past is never dead.
It's not even past.

—William Faulkner

In 2002, almost six decades after the fighting had ended in the Solomons, Dr. Robert Ballard—the oceanographer and explorer who discovered the wreck of the RMS *Titanic*—returned to the Solomons with the goal of locating the wreck of PT 109 in Blackett Strait. Traveling with him was William "Bud" Liebenow, who commanded PT 157, the boat that rescued Jack and his crew off Olasana Island. Also along for the journey was Matthew Maxwell "Max" Kennedy, son of Robert F. Kennedy, Jack's younger brother.

While touring the Pacific, Max Kennedy met with Biuku Gasa and Eroni Kumana, who were both almost eighty years old. Max was the first member of the Kennedy family to meet

Eroni Kumana and Biuku Gasa together again in 2002.

with either of the former scouts. Biuku Gasa's nephew and grandson made a new dugout canoe as a gift for the expedition to take back to America. "I'm making this canoe," Biuku explained, "so people in Washington can come look. So people will hear about the late President Kennedy. So people will remember what happened here. This is my canoe and I make it for the memorial of J. F. Kennedy, from Biuku Gasa."

Eroni Kumana built a private memorial made of stone, standing over seven feet tall, overlooking the sea on his home island of Ranongga, and dedicated it to Kennedy. "When I heard he became president," Eroni said, "in the way of my tradition, I appointed him into the position of chief. As chief he decreed, I will send someone among my people to reach the moon. So it happened! . . . The flag still sits on the moon as the president dreamed it would be. So the chiefship of Kennedy will remain here even after I die, strong as ever, as hard as this rock. I always am thinking of him."

Biuku Gasa sits in a canoe he made as a gift to the United States in memory of John F. Kennedy and the PT 109 story.

AMBASSADOR CAROLINE KENNEDY

Jack Kennedy's only daughter, Caroline, was appointed by President Barack Obama as ambassador to Japan in 2013, where she served until January of 2017. In one of her first official acts as ambassador, she visited the Imperial Palace and met Emperor Akihito to present her credentials. Akihito's father was Emperor Hirohito, who had reigned over Japan before and during World War II, but was also the key figure who decided to surrender to the Allies in

President Kennedy and Caroline Kennedy, photographed on August 25, 1963.

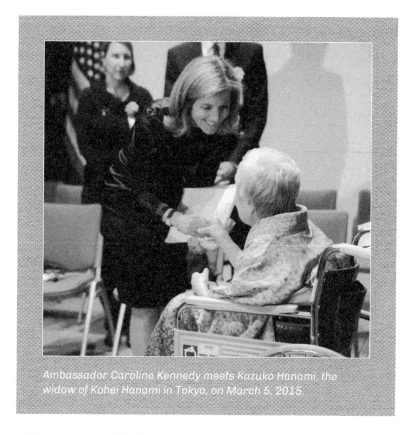

Ambassador Caroline Kennedy meets Kazuko Hanami, the widow of Kohei Hanami in Tokyo, on March 5, 2015.

1945 and reestablished Japan among modern nations.

In March of 2015, Caroline attended a special display at Japan's national archives, "JFK: His Life and Legacy," which featured President Kennedy's service in World War II, his relationship with Japan, and his accomplishments in the White House. Among the artifacts on loan from the John F. Kennedy Presidential Library and Museum in Boston were the letters exchanged between Jack and Captain Hanami, plus the famous coconut message and documents from

Japanese prime minister Ikeda's 1961 visit to the United States.

One of the special guests was an elderly lady seated in a wheelchair and dressed in a beautiful kimono. She was Mrs. Hanami, the widow of the late captain Kohei Hanami. After the opening ceremony, Caroline shook hands with her, saying, "I've been hoping to meet you ever since I became ambassador." It was a true honor for both women to meet each other. The friendship and respect that grew between Hanami and Jack Kennedy became a genuine symbol of peace and goodwill between the United States and Japan after World War II as both countries faced new and difficult challenges.

In 2008, knowing he was nearing the end of his own life, Eroni Kumana wanted to pay his respects to Kennedy. He asked an American friend to deliver a treasured heirloom to the Kennedy family and requested it be placed on Jack's grave. The gift was a prized piece of bakia, or "shell money," a traditional form of currency made of giant clamshells, fashioned into a ceremonial bracelet. It was the traditional symbol of a chief in the Solomons.

That request was carried out on November 1, 2008, at a ceremony held at Arlington National Cemetery. Members of President Kennedy's family gathered to receive Eroni's tribute, which was placed on the grave. It is now on display at the John F. Kennedy Presidential Library and Museum in Boston, next to the famous coconut shell that led to the rescue of JFK and his PT 109 crew.

John F. Kennedy's grave at Arlington National Cemetery, VA, and the ceremonial bracelet gift of honor from Eroni Kumana (inset).

★ AFTER THE WAR ★

Joseph P. Kennedy Jr. was awarded the Distinguished Flying Cross, the Air Medal, and the navy's second-highest decoration awarded for valor in combat—the Navy Cross. A year after his death, the navy launched a destroyer named after him, the USS *Joseph P. Kennedy Jr.* (DD-850). His body was never recovered.

Biuku Gasa lived out his days at his home at Vavudu Village, Kauvi Island, in the Western Solomons. After the war, Gasa and his wife, Nelma, had six children. He was recognized as a patriarch (family leader) by the people of his island. Biuku Gasa died on November 23, 2005, the day after the forty-second anniversary of Kennedy's assassination.

Eroni Kumana lived the rest of his life at his home village of Kongu on the island of Ranongga. He passed away on August 2, 2014, at the age of ninety-three—seventy-one years to the day that PT 109 was sunk in Blackett Strait. Eroni named his youngest son John F. Kennedy. He is survived by nine children, and their families.

Robert Francis "Bobby" Kennedy served as U.S. Attorney General under his brother and President Lyndon B. Johnson until September 1964. He became the junior senator from New York in 1965 until he was assassinated on June 6, 1968.

At the time of his death, Robert was a leading candidate for the Democratic nomination for the presidency in the 1968 election. He is buried at Arlington National Cemetery next to the John F. Kennedy Eternal Flame grave site.

Jacqueline Lee "Jackie" Kennedy Onassis married the Greek millionaire Aristotle Onassis in 1968. After his death in 1975, she returned to New York City and worked as a book editor. Until her passing on May 19, 1994, she remained a lifelong patron of the arts and contributed to the preservation of historic buildings. She remains one of the most admired First Ladies in history.

John Fitzgerald Kennedy Jr. grew up to be a lawyer and was considering a life of public service when he was killed in a plane crash on July 16, 1999, off the coast of Martha's Vineyard. He was buried at sea by his uncle Ted Kennedy, from the navy destroyer USS *Briscoe*.

Caroline Bouvier Kennedy served as U.S. ambassador to Japan for President Barack Obama from 2013 to 2017. She is a likely candidate to run for the Senate or the House of Representatives in 2018, following in the footsteps of her late uncle Senator Robert F. Kennedy.

Kohei Hanami took up farming after the war and, like Kennedy, became a public official for his home village of Shiokawa, in the Fukushima prefecture of Japan. He was elected mayor in 1962.

Gerard Emil Zinser stayed in the navy after World War II, until his retirement in 1957 with the rank of chief petty officer. He returned to Florida, where he worked for the United States Postal Service. He was the last surviving member of the PT 109 crew from the night it was sunk, passing away on August 21, 2001, in Orange Park, Florida. He is buried at Arlington National Cemetery in Virginia.

John E. Maguire moved to Jacksonville, Florida, after the war. When Kennedy was elected president, he appointed Maguire to the post of U.S. Marshal, Southern Florida District. John passed away on December 20, 1990, in Ponte Vedra, Florida, at the age of seventy-four. He is buried at the H. Warren Smith Memorial Cemetery in Jacksonville Beach, Florida.

George Henry Robertson "Barney" Ross came home from the war and entered the insurance business in Barrington, Illinois. President Kennedy asked Ross to help him with his Committee on Juvenile Delinquency and Youth Crime and the formation of the Peace Corps. Ross would also appear in the 1963 Hollywood film *PT 109* as the crusty chief petty officer. Ross died on July 24, 1983, at the age of sixty-three in Washington, DC.

Patrick Henry "Pop" McMahon survived his burns and volunteered to remain at the PT base at Tulagi working on PT engines. He left the navy in 1945 and later served as postmaster with the United States Postal Service in Cathedral City, California. He died on February 18, 1990, in Encinitas, California. He is buried at the Riverside National Cemetery in California.

Raymond Lee "Ray" Starkey returned from the war and worked for the Signal Oil & Gas Field in Huntington Beach, California. Raymond passed away on October 8, 1970, in Anaheim, California.

Leonard Jay Thom was given command of PT 60 after the PT 109 ordeal and also commanded PT 587, which his crew nicknamed the "Thomcat." The "Blond Viking" married his sweetheart in June 1944 and returned from the Pacific in 1946 to start a new life with her in Youngstown, Ohio. On October 6, 1946, the car he was driving was struck by a passing train. It was reported that he turned the wheel the moment before impact so the train would not crush his two passengers. He refused medical help until they were rescued. Len died the next day. Jack Kennedy was a pallbearer (someone who helps carry the casket) at his funeral. Thom is buried at Calvary Cemetery in Youngstown, Ohio.

Andrew Jackson Kirksey has his name inscribed on a list of the missing at the American Cemetery in Manila. Andrew's widow, Kloye, and their son, Jack, met Kennedy while he was campaigning for president in 1960. Kennedy helped Kloye over the years and made sure her son made it through college.

Harold William Marney also has his name inscribed on a list of the missing at the American Cemetery in Manila. Kennedy met his parents when he returned from the Pacific in 1944. In 2014, the collection of John F. Kennedy letters to the Marney family sold for $200,000 at auction in Boston.

The Solomon Islands were granted independence from Great Britain on July 7, 1978, but the people elected to keep their allegiance to Queen Elizabeth II as the ceremonial head of state. In September 2012, the Duke and Duchess of Cambridge (William and Kate) visited the islands to mark the sixtieth anniversary of the accession of Queen Elizabeth II. The National Parliament of the Solomons in the capital of Honiara, on the island of Guadalcanal, was built with foreign aid given by the United States.

RESTORED PT BOATS IN THE UNITED STATES

There are very few World War II–era PT boats remaining today. At the end of the war, most of the boats in the Pacific were shepherded to the island of Samar in the Philippines, stripped of any valuable equipment, and set ablaze on the beach. Some were given to Allied nations who helped win the war. Many that were waiting to be shipped overseas were sold to the highest bidder in 1945. Most of the museum boats that remain come from this group of lucky survivors.

PT 617 is the only remaining example of an Elco-built PT boat currently on display in the world. It was completed at the end of the war and served as a training vessel in Florida. It was restored over the course of five years by PT Boats, Inc. and put on display at Battleship Cove, in Fall River, Massachusetts, in 1986. As the only remaining eighty-foot Elco, PT 617 is the closest example of what PT 109 would have looked like. www.battleshipcove.org/

PT 796 is a seventy-eight-foot Higgins boat nicknamed the "Tail Ender" because she was the last boat of her type produced by the company. She missed taking part in World War II and served as a testing boat in Florida to develop equipment for a new generation of swift boats serving in Vietnam. PT 796 was used in President Kennedy's inaugural parade on January 20, 1961, repainted to appear as PT 109. She was restored to her original configuration and has been on display at Battleship Cove since 1975.

www.battleshipcove.org/

Other boats:

PT 658 in Portland, Oregon:

www.savetheptboatinc.com/

PT 305 in New Orleans, Louisiana:

www.nww2m.com/category/pt-305-update/

PT 728 "Thomcat" in Port Clinton, Ohio:

www.libertyaviationmuseum.org

PT 309 in Fredericksburg, Texas:

www.pacificwarmuseum.org

"Oh, my God! There are sharks out there!" That was my reaction as a high school student, reading Robert Donovan's classic account *PT 109* for the first time. I remember flipping the pages as fast as I could as Jack Kennedy swam out into Ferguson Passage at night (when we all know sharks come out for dinner) to try to signal an American boat for rescue. It was hard to believe such courage existed, yet it was all true. Much later I discovered that same act of valor inspired Pulitzer Prize–winning author John Hersey to write his epic account of the PT 109 story, "Survival."

I hail from the landlocked farmlands of the Southern Tier of New York State. Visiting the ocean as a child was about the most exotic vacation we had back then, short of Disneyland. Sharks were a fascination of mine in the same way kids in New York City must think about king cobras or tigers. They were mysterious, scary, and thankfully, far away. And yet, our family history has strong ties to a maritime past, so it feels like the ocean is in my blood.

My grandfather on my mom's side was a British Merchant Marine officer during World War II who taught navigation and signals to young cadets. On my dad's side, his father worked for the Weir Group in Glasgow, Scotland, where he once served as an engineer aboard the RMS *Queen Mary* for a wartime transatlantic run to New York. Twenty-five years earlier, during World War I, he was working at sea on a warship's pumps when the vessel was suddenly called into action for the Battle of Jutland. My grandfather got to participate in one of the greatest naval clashes in history without an invitation.

Twenty years after reading Donovan's classic book, I watched in awe as Dr. Robert Ballard led a *National Geographic* expedition to locate the wreck of PT 109 in 1,200 feet of water at the bottom of Blackett Strait. Just as fascinating were the two Melanesian scouts who found Jack Kennedy and his crew, Biuku Gasa and Eroni Kumana. Mostly forgotten by outsiders, they had singlehandedly rescued the man who would become our thirty-fifth president from certain death.

Jack Kennedy, with his fellow officers and crew, persevered against the odds to escape with their lives after the loss of PT 109. Jack was fortunate that the story was eventually recorded by a talented writer, John Hersey. Without Hersey's account of the heroic saga, Jack Kennedy would likely never have become president of the United States— the story made him famous nationwide and won him political fortune.

Today, nearly seventy-five years after World War II, the PT 109 story remains with those who lived through

Kennedy's times, but for younger generations it has largely gone untold. Students learn about John F. Kennedy as president, and how he tragically died. But they don't often learn about the single greatest event in his young life that defined the man he would become. This book is an attempt to correct that trend.

Some may ask if a new book on the PT 109 saga is necessary. I feel strongly that famous historical stories are worth retelling when a new generation of young people can learn about the past. Jack Kennedy and the PT 109 disaster is one of the greatest true stories of survival to come out of World War II. It shows the meaning of courage, duty, and sacrifice. And it deserves to be remembered.

★ RECOMMENDED READING ★

I Am #9: John F. Kennedy by Grace Norwich

John F. Kennedy: America's 35th President by Kieran Doherty

The Assassination of President John F. Kennedy by Wil Mara

"The President Has Been Shot!": The Assassination of John F. Kennedy by James L. Swanson

Who Was John F. Kennedy? by Yona Zeldis McDonough, illustrated by Jill Weber

PT 109: John F. Kennedy in World War II by Robert J. Donovan

★ SOURCES ★

Ballard, Robert D., and Michael Hamilton Morgan. *Collision with History: The Search for John F. Kennedy's PT 109.* Washington, DC: National Geographic, 2002.

Blair Jr., Clay and Joan. *The Search for J.F.K.* New York: Berkley, Putnam, 1976.

Breuer, William. *Devil Boats: The PT War against Japan.* Novato: Presidio Press, 1987.

Bulkley, Robert J., *At Close Quarters: PT Boats in the United States Navy.* Washington, DC: Naval History Division, 1962.

Christ, James F. *Mission Raise Hell: The U.S. Marines on Choiseul, October–November 1943.* Annapolis: Naval Institute Press, (reprint) 2006.

Dallek, Robert. *An Unfinished Life: John F. Kennedy, 1917–1963.* New York: Little, Brown and Company, 2003.

Donovan, Robert J. *PT 109: John F. Kennedy in World War II.* New York: McGraw-Hill, 1961.

Doyle, William. *PT 109: An American Epic of War, Survival, and the Destiny of John F. Kennedy.* New York: William Morrow, 2015.

Fay Jr., Paul B. *The Pleasure of His Company.* New York: Harper & Row, 1966.

Gasa, Biuku. "This Is the Story of Captain Kennedy." Typed Manuscript, Kauvi Island, Western Solomon Islands, c. 1960–1961. Translated by (Rev.) E. C. Leadley.

Goodwin, Doris Kearns. *The Fitzgeralds and the Kennedys: An American Saga.* New York: Simon & Schuster, 1987.

Graham, James W. Victura: *The Kennedys, a Sailboat, and the Sea.* Lebanon: ForeEdge (University Press of New England), 2014.

Hamilton, Nigel. *JFK: Reckless Youth.* New York: Random House, 1992.

Hersey, John. *Of Men and War.* New York: Scholastic Book Services, 1963. Includes a revised version of the narrative that Hersey originally wrote for *The New Yorker.*

Keating, Bern. *The Mosquito Fleet: The History of the PT Boat in World War II.* New York: Scholastic Book Services, 1963.

Kennedy, Edward M. *True Compass: A Memoir.* New York: Hachette Book Group, 2009.

Kennedy Smith, Jean. *The Nine of Us: Growing Up Kennedy.* New York: Harper Collins, 2016.

Kennedy, Rose Fitzgerald. *Times to Remember.* New York: Doubleday, 1974.

Keresey, Dick. "Farthest Forward." *American Heritage,* July/August 1998, pp. 60–73.

Keresey, Dick. *PT 105.* Annapolis: Naval Institute Press, 1996.

Leff, Deborah. "A Conversation with PT Boat Veterans." John F. Kennedy Presidential Library and Museum, symposium on June 27, 2005.

May, Stephen J. *Michener's South Pacific.* Gainesville: University Press of Florida, 2011.

Nasaw, David. *The Patriarch: The Remarkable Life and Turbulent Times of Joseph P. Kennedy.* New York: The Penguin Press, 2012.

O'Donnell, Kenneth P., and David F. Powers. *Johnny, We Hardly Knew Ye.* New York: Little Brown and Company, 1972.

Renehan Jr., Edward J. *The Kennedys at War: 1937–1945.* New York: Doubleday, 2002.

Robinson, Ted. *Water in My Veins: The Pauper Who Helped Save a President.* Charleston: CreateSpace, 2012.

Sandler, Martin W. *The Letters of John F. Kennedy.* New York: Bloomsbury, 2013.

Shepard Jr., Tazewell. *John F. Kennedy—Man of the Sea.* New York: William Morrow & Co., 1965.

Thom Kelley, Kate. Recorded interview by Vicki Daitch, September 4, 2003, John F. Kennedy Library Oral History Program.

Tregaskis, Richard. *John F. Kennedy and PT-109.* New York: Random House, 1962.

★ MEDIA SOURCES ★

National Geographic—*The Search for Kennedy's PT-109*, DVD 2004.

Warner Brothers, *PT 109* movie filmed in 1963.

★ PHOTO CREDITS ★

★ INDEX ★

NOTE: Page numbers in *italics* refer to illustrations.

★ ACKNOWLEDGMENTS ★

A special thanks to Deborah Hopkinson and Lisa Sandell; my editor, Paige Hazzan; photo researcher, Amla Sanghvi; my cousin Sandra Morrisette; and to my agent, Fritz Heinzen, for helping me write the best possible book for young readers. In addition, a great debt is owed to Frank J. Andruss Sr., Jack Kirksey, and Ted Walther for sharing their expertise and photographic collections. Thanks to Michael Campbell for his outstanding maps. Thanks also to the great folks at Liberty Aviation Museum in Port Clinton, Ohio, for an outstanding tour of their PT 728 restoration in August 2016. Lastly, a special thank you to my wife, Chona, and her never-ending patience with her history buff husband, and Nanay and Tatay for their constant prayers.

★ ABOUT THE AUTHOR ★

IAIN MARTIN is the author of the young adult nonfiction book, *Gettysburg: The True Account of Two Young Heroes in the Greatest Battle of the Civil War*. He works in publishing, holds an MA in American History from Southern Connecticut State University, and lives in Connecticut, where he specializes in making pancakes for his wife and two kids. He is still terrified of sharks.